HUMAN P
HUMAN VALUE

Towards a society for people as we really are (and not as governments, economists and big corporations would like us to be)

MARTIN WHITLOCK

mh
BOOKS

MINDHENGE BOOKS

ABOUT THE AUTHOR

Martin Whitlock's expertise is in solving problems and making things work. He has applied these skills in business and educational settings, helping to fix organisations that were in danger of losing their way. He has also been hands-on, fixing up old buildings, most notably in the second series of Channel 4's *Grand Designs*. Over the past ten years he has written extensively on politics and the economy, full details of which can be found on his website: www.martinwhitlock.co.uk.

Human Politics : Human Value
First published in 2014 by Mindhenge Books
Green Dragon Barn, Hutcherleigh, Totnes, TQ9 7AD, U.K.
www.mindhenge.co.uk

Copyright © Martin Whitlock 2014

Designed by Francis Porter
www.francisporterdesign.com

Cover design: Martin Whitlock

Printed and bound by CPI Group (UK) Ltd, Croydon, CR0 4YY
ISBN: 978-0-9930167-0-7

British Library Cataloguing in Publication Data.
A catalogue record for this book is available from the British Library.

CONTENTS

CONTENTS

INTRODUCTION

ACROSS THE WEST, the contract between people and the politicians who govern them is unravelling. The discourse of politics has lost its way, with principle and ideology overtaken by public relations and weighed down by the dead hand of a self-serving press. Power seeps away into the boardrooms of multinational companies, where decisions are taken unaccountably that may affect the lives of millions around the globe. In all of this, the capacity of individual people to assert their will and express their freedom is easily lost. Democracy is lauded in name even as the power of people to participate coherently in the decisions that will shape their lives is fading away.

This growing pervasiveness of the state and its surrogates in people's lives arises from the frustration of governments at their inability to bring about effective and useful change. From a management perspective, society is too messy and disordered and the only way to move it forward is to get it organised and under control. No one can say – in Britain, at least – that the attempt has not been made. At every level of political engagement there are targets, thresholds, inspectors, standards, identity checks, databases, statutory returns, regulations, regulatory bodies and innumerable previously un-thought-of ways of breaking the law, all conceived of as necessary and desirable tools to make society manageable.

The results, predictably, have not been happy. If the management of a diverse society of human beings is necessarily a frustrating process, the failure of all these tools to create contentment is doubly frustrating for the people who wield them. Frustration is rapidly becoming – and in many areas has become already – the defining characteristic of political engagement. It infects everybody, from governments who are frustrated at their failure to achieve the good things that will make them popular, to the people whose lives are touched by the consequences of that failure and are frustrated by their powerlessness in the face of it. Where government policy is delivered, in local government, schools, hospitals and the vast array of government and private agencies delivering services from the public purse, the frustration is palpable. Life at this level is a permanent struggle to satisfy two competing sets of demands: the immediate and often simple needs of the users of the services and the complicated and contradictory "delivery frameworks" enacted by government.

Observing all of this is the army of journalists, writers and broadcasters who, obliged in the sleepless media to make instant sense of it all and frustrated by the lack of a consistent narrative, resort to speculation, simplification, alarmism and personalisation, in a bid for any sort of coherence, whether true or fanciful. Their stories are fed to them by legions of policy advisors, think-tanks, campaigning organisations, specialists, scientists and all sorts of self-created and appointed experts – including ordinary people with opinions – who, as well as being frustrated, are also bewildered, unable to understand why it should prove so difficult to give effect to whatever policy solution each one feels is self-evidently the right thing to do.

Human Politics : Human Value analyses the frustration and points to its cause, in the form of an economy in which so much work has no productive or useful value. It proposes a route back from this oppressive powerlessness in which the first step for both people and politicians is to re-assert the individual will as the driving force of collaborative endeavour.

A NOTE ON THE TEXT

FREQUENT REFERENCES TO "the west" may seem slightly archaic, since the term begins to embrace developed democracies across the globe, but its use is intended to recollect that the "western democracies" represent a paradigm of governance to which the rest of the world is encouraged to conform. Paradigm failure is a sure pre-cursor to systemic failure, which is a way of saying that, if the western democracies continue to fail, the very currency of democracy in the world will be debased and alternative systems will emerge to displace it.

For a similar reason, although this book is chiefly concerned with conditions in Great Britain, the centrality of British power, institutions and language in framing the terms both of western democracy and of market capitalism means that what happens in Britain continues to have disproportionate global resonance. If Great Britain created the modern world, there is a fair chance that it will be in Britain that the full effects of market implosion will first be felt. The accumulating effect of a forty year crisis in British politics suggests that this may now be happening before our eyes.

Chapter 1

HOW RICH WAS MR DARCY?

The evolution of the wealth divide in the industrial age

MR DARCY, THE smouldering romantic hero who put the "pride" into Jane Austen's novel *Pride and Prejudice*, had an income of £10,000 a year. Combined with his youth and handsome appearance, this made him one of the most eligible bachelors of his time. His friend, Mr Bingley, was scarcely less eligible with an income of only half that amount. Mr Bennet, the father of the novel's heroine, had £2,000 a year to keep his wife and five daughters in a respectable style, and famously managed to accumulate no savings. The richest real person in Britain at the close of the 18th century was probably the Duke of Bridgewater, the canal pioneer. His income is said to have approached £100,000 a year at its peak.

What do these figures mean in the modern world? The answer depends on whether you look at prices or earnings. Consumer prices rose about 90 times between 1797[1] and 2013, by which time Mr Darcy would have needed £900,000 to buy what his income would originally have brought him[2]. Earnings and productivity, however, have risen far more, so a man of Mr Darcy's economic status would have had an income of over £13 million in 2013. Mr Bennet would have had £2.6 million a year, which, with expenditure of only £180,000, would leave plenty of scope to persuade worthless young men to marry one or other of his daughters.

---

1   *Pride and Prejudice* was written in 1796 – 97, but not published until 1813.
2   All calculations derived from Lawrence H. Officer and Samuel H. Williamson, *Five Ways to Compute the Relative Value of a UK Pound Amount, 1270 to Present*, MeasuringWorth, 2014.

The income of the third Duke of Bridgewater – about £130 million a year at 2013 values – would suggest a fortune in the range of £2 to 3 billion. This enormous sum would be nowhere near enough to have made him the richest person in Britain in 2013; for that, according to *The Sunday Times Rich List*, he would have needed over £13 billion, while at £3 billion he would have struggled to make it into the top 20. He would not even have been the richest duke: that honour belongs to the Duke of Westminster, whose property empire was estimated to be worth nearly £8 billion in 2013. History, it would seem, has been kind to the super-rich; because incomes have risen so much faster than prices, they can buy far more while spending proportionately less of their income. This means that, if they invest successfully, they can accumulate wealth even more rapidly than before.

At the other end of the earnings range, the comparison is quite different. Consider the case of Abel, a worker on one of Mr Darcy's farms, who earned about £30 a year in 1797[1]. With this he managed to support his wife, Bessie, and their two children. What Abel and Bessie could buy for £30 would have cost Steve and Jayne, their modern counterparts, about £2,700 at 2013 prices, by which time, if Steve's economic status had kept pace with the average, he should have been on nearly £40,000 a year. In fact, he earned half that. According to government figures, the average farm worker's wage for 2013 was about £20,000.

This shortfall is part of a pattern. It applies to both manual and professional occupations. Indeed, one of the reasons why modern society is generally more equal than that of the 18th century is that the pay gap between the "middle class" and the "working class" has narrowed, while large numbers of very low paid jobs (such as domestic service) have disappeared. That phrase "generally more equal", however, disguises the fact that people with established wealth have done much better. While the 18th century Mr Darcy had an income 330 times that of his farm worker, someone similarly wealthy in the

---

1   Williamson J.G., *The Structure of Pay in Britain, 1710-1911, Research in Economic History*, 7 (1982).

21st century would be more than 600 times richer than the labourers he employs.

Earnings have outstripped prices because technology has enabled each person to do far more work. Abel walked behind a horse, whereas Steve drives a tractor and can do the work of a dozen Abels. So even though Steve's wages have not risen as much as they should have done, he and Jayne still have far more to spend than Abel and Bessie could ever dream of. But how much more? If Abel and Bessie could get by on £30 a year, Steve and Jayne ought to be able to live to the same basic standard on £2,700, in which case their actual income of £20,000 should leave them feeling nearly eight times richer. In fact, on that income, Steve, Jayne and their children will be living in poverty, while £2,700 is nowhere near enough to sustain any sort of existence. So Steve's family are not eight times better off that Abel's. Comparing 18th century lifestyles with those of today is an inexact science, to say the least, and the welfare state has made a big difference, but at a rough estimate they might be twice as well off, or three times at best.

History has dealt Steve and Jayne a double whammy. Steve's earnings have not kept up with the average increase in wealth over two centuries, and the increase that he has received is not reflected in their standard of living. Their situation is far from unique; it is shared by the majority of their fellow-workers. Visitors to Britain's stately homes, or those who view the past through the prism of television costume dramas, will certainly be surprised to learn that in modern Britain the wealthiest people are even wealthier than they were two hundred years ago. The opulence of those houses and the armies of servants that ran them are, however, part of the answer to this conundrum. In those days the rich spent their money openly to maintain their status, and many landed families fell into decline by spending more than they could afford. The modern rich are more discreet; they have gained their wealth by investing in profitable assets which are generally far less tangible and much better concealed.

COMPARISONS ACROSS THE centuries are inherently difficult. The underlying picture, however, is incontrovertible. Since industrialisation took hold of Britain in the early 19th century, productivity has increased vastly, making far more wealth per capita that before, but the distribution of that wealth has favoured capital investors over paid employees. Incomes have risen unequally, so workers are less well off than they could be, in addition to which the effective spending power of income, its "useful" spending power, has increased far less than gross productivity.

Effective spending is spending on things that people want; it turns their income into real wealth or wellbeing – the stuff that improves the quality of people's lives and allows them to flourish. Effective spending power has increased much more slowly than overall consumer spending because the great developments in productivity that allowed wages to rise have been accompanied by inefficiencies in the economic system that require useless spending. If the economy of today was as efficient as that of 1797, then £2,700 really would be enough for a family to get by. In fact it is much less efficient, and this has a far bigger impact on the less well off, for whom a higher proportion of their income goes upon their basic needs. For the already wealthy, it works to their advantage, as we shall see.

For a picture of this, watch Jayne and Steve as they set off for their weekly shopping. First they have to get there: they can either walk half a mile to catch the occasional bus or take their battered estate car. Motorised transport of any sort is an improvement on Abel and Bessie's options; they invariably had to walk. But the distances are greater, too; the shops in the village have long since closed down and there are few alternatives to the large supermarket on the town's edge, twelve miles away. Either way, the transport is expensive. At £5 each for a round trip on the bus, the car certainly seems a cheaper option, but only because its overheads are already paid for.

At the supermarket the parking is free, although how free it really is Steve and Jayne don't stop to consider. Presumably several acres of shiny tarmac spread over prime development land does not come cheap. Here is an invisible cost that they will pay for as their shopping is rung through the till. The same goes for the enormous building, and the dozens of staff. All this infrastructure does no more than connect an item arriving in a lorry at one end of the car park with a customer arriving in a car at the other. Boxes are unloaded from the lorry, separated out, stock-checked, placed in store, wheeled out to the aisles, unpacked onto the shelves and priced up. The customer then reverses the process, picking items off the shelves into their trolley and negotiating through checkout and bag-packing staff. All of this is cost, coming straight out of Steve and Jayne's already modest income.

Once they reach the shelves, these intermediate costs continue to mount. Almost every item is surrounded with packaging; over their lifetimes they will buy tonnes of cardboard and plastic, and then pay once again through their local taxes to have it taken away in their rubbish bins. Greater still is all the transport they are buying; nobody expects to have bananas in England unless they have travelled far, but potatoes from Egypt? Apples from California, or New Zealand? Even the carrots have come from four hundred miles away, and this despite the fact that the farm where Steve works produces carrots commercially. Livestock travels across Europe in tightly packed lorries, often spending only a short time in the place where the label says it comes from; processed food thunders up and down the motorways and even goods produced locally will have been on a journey. Supermarkets manage their wares out of central depots, so local products may have travelled half way across the country *and back* before finding their place on the shelves.

Consider, as they load the bags into the car, what proportion of the money that they handed over at the checkout represents the actual food content of their purchases – the part that Jayne, Steve and their family will actually eat, and which will enable them to flourish. Strip away the car park, the building, the staff, the lighting, the fridges and freezers, the fancy tills, the packaging and the lorries, planes and ships, and you are left with what? Supermarkets aim for about 30% gross margin, which means that nearly a third of the bill is for running the shop and taking a shareholder profit. But the wholesalers and intermediaries that supply the supermarkets take their profit, too, on top of which there is all that packaging and transport to be paid for. All that adds up to another third, while the costs of food processing add more again. On average, the farmer will see less than 20%. The rest disappears in a costly and convoluted journey from producer to plate.

Abel and Bessie may not have eaten bananas but their food came from much closer to home. Their staples were dairy and grains – mainly oats on Mr Darcy's Derbyshire estate – a sustaining if monotonous local diet supplemented by whatever the family could grow for itself. Productivity may have been low, but the efficiency of the path from production to consumption was exceedingly high. With most of their food coming direct from the producer, they incurred very little additional cost. Almost all of the work that went into the product was capable of being usefully consumed.

The food the supermarket sells may or may not be nicer than Bessie's home cooking; it is certainly much more varied, it may be more plentiful and more convenient, and it may even be healthier in some respects (although, depending upon the choices Steve and Jayne make, it may be far less healthy). Since its production is mechanised and highly efficient, Steve and Jayne should be able to afford much more than Bessie and Abel could – as much as thirteen times more, based on the average increase in productivity, leaving them plenty of money to buy other things. The fact that they can't – that they have no spare money and are still not able to make the choices they would like when buying their food – goes to the heart of the economic challenges that society is facing in the modern age.

HOW CAN A system of food distribution that adds 400% to farm-gate prices be considered "good value", as the big supermarkets clearly are? Because they encourage us to overlook the crucial distinction between wealth and cost when we make our purchasing decisions. The misunderstanding is wrapped up in the phrase "cost of living". The requirements to sustain life are not cost, but wealth. Wealth is wellbeing; it is what we live by: it allows us to flourish. The production and nurturing of wealth is, therefore, not a cost or a tax on life, but the primary purpose and activity of life itself.

The components of wealth are many and diverse: in addition to the essentials of air, water, food, warmth, shade and shelter, they include good health, effective relationships and a sound emotional state and a lengthy list of desirables embracing education, books, television, mobile phones, fitted kitchens, country walks, the natural environment and the time to enjoy all these and many other things. Central to all of this are the rewards and benefits of thought and feeling: empathy, love, creativity, ideas and a sense of wonder. Everything we want to use or consume, experience, do or have done for us, that imparts such benefits and allows us to live fulfilled, satisfying lives, is wealth. Making, nurturing and sharing wealth is what we, as human beings, do.

Work is any engagement or activity that contributes to the making, nurturing and sharing of wealth. To illustrate this, we talk of working at our relationships, working in the garden, working on our physical fitness, as well as in the reductive sense of working to earn money. Productive, useful, life-enhancing work is what people are designed to do; they want to do it and it allows them to flourish. To talk about work as a cost of staying alive is to reduce life to a vegetative state, or to misunderstand the nature of being. Not being able to work, on the other hand, is a cost, since it means leading a diminished life. Similarly, working too much at something, beyond the point that it is life-enhancing, may lead to illness, depression or social harm.

Unproductive work is also a huge cost. This is work that should be unnecessary, and which displaces useful, life-enhancing work. Everybody's life is diminished by this. Indeed, since work is wealth-production, "unproductive work" is a contradiction in terms; but because a modern economy is so packed with unproductive activity it has given work a bad name as the thing that depletes and exhausts people, rather than enhancing their lives. For many people, therefore, work has indeed become cost, not adding to the total of wanted, productive activity but obstructing, harming or devaluing it. For Jayne and Steve, the cost of their £50 trolley-load of food is not the nourishment it contains but the £35 or more of supply chain costs that have attached themselves to it along the way.

Despite this immense cost-surcharge, Jayne and Steve still find the supermarket the cheapest place to source their food. This is partly because it is almost the only place: the town has a small butcher and a greengrocer, but the general grocers are long gone. Four super-market brands in Britain control over three quarters of the grocery market; a handful of other brands control much of the rest. For most, the old model of "pile it high and sell it cheap" is long gone; retail margins (the difference between the price they buy for and the price at which they sell) are on average higher than those of a corner shop or smaller convenience store. The economies of scale do not arise because the huge shops with their vast car parks are cheaper to run, but because the price they pay to the producers is significantly lower. In overseas producer countries as well as on farms in Britain, super-markets insist upon the lowest possible prices for the produce they buy, and because they control almost the entire retail food market, they get their way. If a corner shop could buy its stock for the price the supermarkets pay, it could undercut them and still make its own-ers a comfortable living.

The supermarkets are skilled at creating an impression of good val-ue, mixing low-price offers and apparent bargains with much more profitable items elsewhere on their shelves. Cheap, basic products sit alongside more expensive alternatives: the cheap ones create an expectation that the more expensive ones are better quality or more desirable; the expensive ones make the cheap ones seem good value. In neither case is there much relationship between price and content: white flour (although more highly processed) is cheaper that whole-meal; bread may be scarcely more expensive than the flour required to make it, despite its being bulkier, more easily damaged and much more perishable than flour in its raw state. It is commonly cheaper to buy processed food than the raw ingredients required to prepare it. When it comes to fruit and vegetables, supermarkets create a prob-lem called "expensive fresh produce" and solve it by providing cheap processed alternatives, the bright packaging of which conceals a poorer nutritional content.

People who take on the work of cooking their own meals pay higher prices for the ingredients, effectively subsidising the low prices of the industrial food processors. Bessie prepared food from raw ingredients, but it makes more sense for Jayne to take part-time paid work, if she can get it, and use her earnings to buy cheaper, processed food. It "makes sense", that is, in the economic counter-reality in which the supermarket supply chain is considered "more efficient" than the pre-industrial alternative of local farmers selling their produce in the town market. True efficiency in distribution comes from connecting the producer and the consumer as closely as possible, yet the range of clean, good-looking, often pre-packaged fresh produce that supermarkets display can only be achieved through a complex supply chain, the effect of which is to keep the producer and the consumer firmly apart.

Size is crucial to the supermarkets' business model in allowing them to control prices; but it is also the source of their biggest cost, which is the complexity and scale of their distribution systems. Keeping this cost down while maintaining sales volume is the key to their success, and it is only low wages that make the model viable. Lorry drivers, meat packers, poultry pluckers, potato washers, fork lift operators, shelf stackers, trolley handlers, till operators, cleaners and myriad other activities within the food supply industry all command low levels of pay, and because the supermarkets are such large employers their low wages become normalised, spreading out into other areas of the economy, including the people who make or grow the real wealth that the supermarkets trade.

Carrots that have been carefully selected (with a high proportion rejected), trucked to a processing centre, washed, trimmed, bagged and chilled, then trucked again to distribution centres en route to the individual stores, should be far more expensive than those just dug from the ground and sold untrimmed in a farm shop or a local market. Economic logic insists this should be so, because of all the extra work involved in production. If people's spending money arises from the work that they do, then shopping is the trading of their own work for the things that they buy. The more work contained in those things, the

more of their work they should have to give to obtain them, and shoppers ought to be able to decide how much of somebody else's work
they want to pay for and how much they want to do for themselves.

In general, however, all that washing, trimming, bagging and
trucking does not add as much to the price as it should. There are
cheaper outlets, but not *so* much cheaper. A carrot is a carrot, more
or less: it has a certain value to a consumer; it sustains life to a certain extent. The price the supermarket can charge has to include both
that innate value and the cost of its own processing and distribution chain. The fact that the resulting price is anywhere near that of
muddy, unselected carrots in a farm shop does not reflect an efficient
use of work but the low value placed on that work. This includes the
work of growing the carrots in the first place: the grower is paying
indirectly for the supply chain and the retail infrastructure through
the low price that supermarkets pay for products at the farm gate.
Steve's farm supplies carrots to a supermarket chain, so he is subsidising the price of his trolley-full of shopping with the low wage he is
paid as a direct consequence of their trading model.

FROM CARROTS TO bananas to everything else, the work of generating the wellbeing that allows people to flourish is subject to costs
that dilute its value – costs much greater than they were in Abel
and Bessie's time. Some are necessary, but the mechanism that ought
naturally to minimise them seems to have the opposite effect. The
mechanism is efficiency, which is nothing more complicated than the
measure of effort made relative to useful product. Where effort made
is all the work that people do, both paid and unpaid, for themselves
and others, both at home and away from it, and product is the things
that bring fulfilment to their lives and enable them to flourish, it
should be easy enough to see what work is useful and what work one
would, ideally, do without. What disrupts this simple calculation is
the tyranny of price, which seeks to displace work as the measure of
efficiency. When the measure of work relative to product is replaced
by the measure of the price of that product, the true value of human
labour ceases to be counted as anything other than another cost.

When the price is low, a supermarket's customers are not invited to consider whether the work of selecting, washing, trimming, bagging, chilling and trucking carrots is useful to them, and whether, therefore, they want to give more of their own work in exchange for it. Instead, they enter into an unspoken bargain in which they trade true, human value for the appearance of profit; in seeking to gain from what appears to be the free labour of selecting, washing, trimming, bagging, chilling and trucking they place in jeopardy the true value of their own productive labour. In this way price distorts the logic of human purpose, substituting for it a competition in which the winners are those for whom profit, rather than useful work and the opportunity to flourish, is the objective.

In 1930 the economist J M Keynes predicted in his *Economic Possibilities for our Grandchildren* that by the early 21st century economic productivity would have risen so far that people would only have to do paid work for fifteen hours a week to maintain a comfortable lifestyle. He was right about the productivity, but wrong about the work. The great rise in productivity that industrialisation has wrought has made labour so plentiful that there is much more incentive to keep down its price than there is to use it sparingly. The way the economy has evolved requires people to work not less but more, as they struggle to make ends meet on low rates of pay. The need for people to earn money means that the supply of labour increases still further, making people even cheaper to employ.

Globalisation has internationalised the labour market, causing businesses to take their activities to countries where the value placed on work is even lower still. In the race for ever-cheaper labour, the idea that work might be undervalued has been completely lost sight of. The model of economic development that emerged in Britain in the 19th century and is now prevalent across the globe actively encourages people to buy the work of others for far, far less than they themselves seek to gain from it. A person may be employed in full time paid work, and yet not earn enough to support a reasonable standard of living. Both conditions are so normal that it could even seem strange to use the word "exploitation" in connection with them; yet they devalue human relationships and undermine the value of work, thereby creating or exacerbating many of the social and economic problems that governments across the world are struggling to solve.

Chapter 2

THE TRANSACTIONAL ECONOMY

The rise and rise of unproductive work

MEASURABLE ECONOMIC OUTPUT per person in Britain in 2010 is estimated to have been about 40 times what it was in the year 1 AD. Of that increase, over 93% has taken place in the last two hundred years. Between 1810 and 2010, output per person increased eleven times, of which 88% has occurred in the second half of *that* period. Nearly 80% of the growth between 1910 and 2010 occurred in the second half of that period, after 1960[1]. Globally, although the overall amount of growth is lower, the pattern is much the same. Measurable economic output per person has grown in the last two centuries at a rapidly increasing rate.

This acceleration in output is an example of cumulative percentage gain. Like compound interest, a fixed percentage increase translates into a ever-greater actual increase over time. To illustrate how it works: £1 invested at 5% compounded over a hundred years increases by 63 pence in the first ten years and £51 in the last ten years. Of the total increase, 91% takes place in the second half of the period.

Cumulative percentage gain is a *geometric progression*, like 1, 2, 4, 8, 16, 32 ..., in which numbers increase by a multiple each time. Provided the multiple is greater than one, the numbers increase at an accelerating rate. Computer processing power has progressed in that way, doubling every year or so as the technology advances. For how long this can continue is uncertain; human patterns of activity do not

---

1   Calculations derived from Bolt, J. and J. L. van Zanden (2013). *The First Update of the Maddison Project; Re-Estimating Growth Before 1820*. Maddison Project Working Paper 4.

naturally operate with continual acceleration. People do not walk upstairs taking the first, second, fourth, eighth and then the sixteenth step, even when they're in a hurry. But they might well take the second, fourth, sixth and eighth steps, i.e. two at a time.

Two at a time is an *arithmetic progression*, like 1, 3, 5, 7, 9 ..., in which the difference between each number is of a similar size. Such a pattern of regular intervals is common in human experience and design, whereas the consequences of a geometric progression can be hard for the human brain to comprehend. Mathematically-minded children like to bamboozle their friends by asking whether they would rather have £1, then £2, then £3 and so on for each day of a month, or a single penny on the first day, two pence on the second, four pence on the third, eight pence on the fourth, and so on. How surprised they are to discover that while the first option adds up to £465, the latter, geometric, sequence produces over £10 million in thirty days!

When an economy grows geometrically at a certain rate, the amount of additional activity every year gets bigger and bigger. If the rate of growth also increases, the amount of growth each year is even bigger still. In Britain, the rate of growth per person in the economy has increased greatly in the last 200 years. The average rate between 1910 and 2010 was, at nearly 2%, more than twice the average of the previous hundred years and only in the 1850s – the high water mark of British power – did it even approach that level during the 19th century. To put that in money terms, allowing for inflation, the average increase in output each year between 1810 and 1910 was about £25 per person, while between 1910 and 2010 it was £180 and in the decade prior to the crash of 2008 it was not far off £600 per person. The effect of this geometric pattern of growth is clearly seen in the graph, which starts slowly but accelerates rapidly in the second half. The amount of additional wealth per person that was being created each year in Britain just prior the the crash was at least ten times what it was at the height of the industrial revolution, when Britain was the world's pre-eminent economic power.

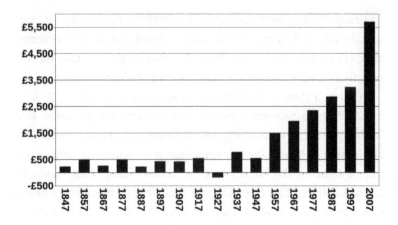

Figure 1: Additional output per person in each decade ending in the given year
(£, adjusted for inflation)

Ought this to surprise us? Or are we so inured to the centrality of economic growth in political discourse that we do not stop to wonder how it is possible for economic output to accelerate at such break-neck speed? Were growth to continue at 2% per year in real terms, and average wages were to keep up with it, by 2100 the average wage would be at least £150,000 in today's money, so people could consume six times as much as they do at present. That is not likely to happen; nor, as Steve's and Jayne's situation shows, has it – or any-thing like it – happened in the last 200 years. As we saw in Chapter 1, Steve and Jayne are nothing like thirteen times better off than Abel and Bessie, their counterparts of 1797, which the figures say is the minimum they should be. Why is it that growth has accelerated at such a colossal rate, and yet the real wealth experienced by ordinary people has increased so much less, even to the point where it has started to decline? The answer lies in a change in the nature of the work that people are paid to do.

IN PRE-INDUSTRIAL TIMES, craftsmen formed guilds and enjoyed high status because they owned their own labour. The investment required was that of gaining an apprenticeship and developing skills;

the rate of work was dictated by an individual's physical capacity to make things by hand and payment came directly through the patronage of individual customers. The producer and the consumer were closely connected through a relationship that matched the capacity of one with the wants of the other.

Industrialisation has broken down that personal relationship. Production is no longer tailored to specific wants but operates instead on the principal of systematic over-supply, creating a wide range from which consumers are encouraged to choose. Capital investment has been substituted for the development of human skills, buying machinery with the capacity to produce at an almost unlimited rate. For decades, factories run almost entirely by machines, with hardly any need for human labour, have been anticipated. The technology to achieve this is well within grasp, and yet, across the world, hundreds of millions of factory workers remain ranged along production lines, performing repetitive physical tasks, often for long hours at low pay and in difficult conditions.

The chief thrust of technological development in the past thirty years or so has not been in the direction of greater mechanisation. Robotisation has had far less impact on people's lives than was once envisaged, and old technologies such as the internal combustion engine, although much improved, are still waiting to be superseded. The big change has been the digital information revolution, made possible by the development of micro-processor technology that provides both the systems and networks to store data, text, music, images, games and films, and the devices on which to play and view them. This technology has created whole new ranges of products, while the pace of its development has led to a constant stream of innovation and upgrades. These seek marginal functional improvements just sufficient to ensure a rapid cycle of device redundancy and new purchases of the latest versions.

The direction technology has taken reflects an economic imperative to increase demand for products rather than to reduce the amount of paid work that people must do to supply their needs. The object is to balance the means of production with the means of consumption, making sure that people are in a position to consume all the things that an economy makes. Consumers have to be able to afford the goods that are produced, and this alone explains why the mechanisation of production has not advanced at anything like the pace of which the technology is capable. Such is the over-supply of labour that it is cheaper to employ people than it is to automate production. The employment of people puts money into their hands, making them potential consumers for the products being made.

The over-supply of labour has, by keeping wages low, discouraged investment in production technology, but productivity is still able to increase as the combination of cheap labour and machinery is fine-tuned to optimum advantage. With a rising global population, and more and more productive activity located in low-wage parts of the world, there is nowhere near enough manufacturing work for people in higher wage parts of the world to do. In the case of Britain, most paid work that can easily be exported has long flown from her shores. Much of what is left relies upon specific expertise or intellectual property, or is un-exportable because (like hairdressing) it requires the worker and the person paying them to be in the same place at the same time.

Recent generations of economists and politicians have made a virtue of this, praising the transformation of Britain over the past thirty years from a manufacturing to a service economy. The idea is that instead of bashing lumps of metal into shape (as the caricature has it) with their hands, Britons are doing intelligent and valuable things in their heads. In the 1980s a picture was painted of a dynamic, new, office and shop-based economy to set against the closing collieries, shipyards and steelworks. More recently, however, the banking crisis has provided evidence of the vulnerability of service-driven growth, provoking calls for a return to the true value of things that are physically made.

This distinction, however, is much less simple than it seems. We talk about *making* a film, or television programme; we use the terms holiday-*making* and re*creation*; and we use the word *creative* to describe all sorts of activities that do not necessarily give rise to a physical product. Hairdressing may be a service, but people know that what they have at the end of it is materially not the same as what they started with; the process is a physical, creative one, using tools to give form and texture to a finished result. The same goes for cooking, cleaning and brain surgery; there is a tangible, material result in each case. Education is also a highly creative process. All good teachers are makers in a deep sense.

These services are all things that people actively want, in the same way that they want food, clothes, shelter and other things that are physically made. Not everything, however, that is physically nurtured or crafted is truly "wanted" in this sense. Steve's and Jayne's supermarket trolley contained quantities of food packaging, all carefully made in a factory and most of which they will throw away. Packaging falls into a different category of things for which people pay. They may acknowledge a need for it, but they do not want more of it than is strictly necessary.

Many services are of this sort. If someone could get through their life without ever paying a penny to a lawyer, they would count it a good result. Nor did anybody ever phone a call centre because they really wanted to. Although financial, legal and accountancy services are a big part of the British economy, nobody wants to buy more of any of them than they can avoid. The price of almost everything contains an amount for business services, including management overheads, advertising, sales and marketing, etc., but if people could buy just the item without paying for these additional services, they would certainly choose to do so. The biggest slice, as we saw with the supermarkets, is found in the distribution chain. Moving goods from where they are to where they are needed is a desirable thing, provided the distance travelled is as little as possible. But the profit margins that are taken by intermediaries at each stage between the farm gate and the kitchen table are added costs that no one would choose to to pay if they could deal with the producer directly.

Management, legal and accountancy costs are part of a sub-category of necessary evils intended to keep an eye on the way that people behave. Business is full of them, and they spill over into many aspects of government, too, from the inspection of schools to traffic regulations to the criminal law. These are things that people accept as needed, but they also know that in an ideal world they would *not* be needed. If people could choose to co-operate with one another, to behave honestly and fairly without having to be made to do so, these costs would not arise.

A more useful distinction, therefore, than that between the manufacturing and the service economy, is that between the economic activity that people actually want, and that which, were it feasible, they would happily avoid. In the first category are products (whether goods or services) that bring authentic wellbeing, nourishing the body, mind and spirit and helping people to flourish. In the second are the costs that operate against this wellbeing, which exist on a scale from "still highly necessary in an imperfect world" to "completely unnecessary and therefore harmful to the general good". Taken collectively, all these necessary and unnecessary costs can be classed together as *transactional activity*. "Transactions" refer to the way in which human activity is organised and managed, rather than the productive wellbeing that such activity is capable of creating.

This explains how growth in the economy has continued to accelerate, even after a two hundred year period of sustained expansion. Industrialisation in the 19th century was about the production of real things, which increased steadily as manufacturing techniques were developed and improved. This growth had physical and material limitations: factories remained labour intensive, even if far less so than the craft skills that they replaced, and were generally dependent upon raw materials still extracted using human labour. The capacity of labour to do more, even with the aid of machines, could only grow at a certain speed. Similarly, the capacity to consume actual goods was limited by people's need or want to do so, and their ability to purchase. This also increased only at a gradual, incremental pace. This, therefore, was the "arithmetical progression" phase of the economy's growth, and until about 1930 the economy grew by a broadly similar amount each decade.

The rapid acceleration in growth since the 1950s, however, and particularly since the "service economy" was heralded in the 1980s, has occurred largely on the strength of a huge increase in transactional activity during that period. Although the rate of increase in truly productive activity is connected to human patterns of behaviour, transactional activity, not having such physical and material limitations, can increase rapidly, in the manner of a geometrical progression, to a near-infinite extent. Once upon a time a person requiring a pair of shoes paid a shoe-maker to make them; the shoe-maker had only to add the value of the materials to the value of his own time. Now, a pair of trainers leaves a factory in Asia for as little as £3, to be sold on a British high street for £80 or more. That £3 already includes transactional costs incurred at source, in addition to the materials and labour. As much as 90% of the price paid by the consumer is not for the productive value of the shoes, but for transactional costs that are introduced along a convoluted route between the maker and the user. Most of these costs are incurred in Britain, and therefore add directly to the sum of British wealth creation as measured by gross domestic product (GDP).

What this tells us is that the explosive growth of the economy has been brought about by including in the measure of economic activity vast quantities of paid work that is at best a necessary evil and at worst completely useless for anything other than making some people rich at the expense of others. Steve (the carrot grower from chapter 1) earns a slice of the economic pie that is relatively thinner than that of Abel (his 18th century predecessor) because so many people have a finger in it who are not real producers. Similarly, of the price of those trainers, £16 has gone to the British government in VAT, another £30 to the retailer, £5 to the wholesaler and maybe £25 to the "maker", who is not, of course, the manufacturer as such but the brand owner who placed the order with a factory in Asia. Each of these has their own costs, all arising from yet more transactional activity such as marketing and sales, distribution, accountancy, premises, financial and legal services, etc. It is even possible that the trainer has been designed in Britain, in which case a small amount of its inherent value does originate in the UK economy. If so, it is the only part that does. Nonetheless, 90% or more of the retail price will go down as British economic production, and will feature in the country's measure of GDP.

TRANSACTIONAL COSTS ARE nothing new. Early farming communities on the Mesopotamian plain produced plenty of grain but had no timber for building, so they traded with communities living on the forested mountains. Among them was Alam, a farmer who found that he had accumulated more surplus grain that his neighbours. He traded it with the foresters for a larger than normal quantity of timber; then, finding he had more than he needed to build his house, he stock-piled the rest to sell on to his neighbours in exchange for their grain. He understood, of course, that because his timber now contained the added value of the transport from the forest, he would need to get more for it than he had paid the foresters; but he found that people would pay him even more than that. There were several other elements of value-added, including immediate availability, security of supply and the opportunity to purchase in small quantities, for which his neighbours would pay an additional price.

Alam was the world's first builders' merchant, and also the world's first capitalist, since he inadvertently used his spare grain as capital to start a business that made him a marginal return, or profit. Apart from the transport, the additional value-added for which his customers were paying did not create additional costs for him, and yet his capacity to hold stock presented him with an economic advantage. Current political and social ideology would commend him for this. He took an entrepreneurial risk by choosing to invest in a business rather than to build himself an even bigger house; he may also appear to have created jobs in the transport sector, although in fact he only re-allocated paid work away from whomever otherwise would have made the journey. By making it easier he may well have increased the volume of two-way trade, and as such he contributed to an increase in GDP. By making a market, however, he exerted control over the rate of exchange between key commodities, maintaining sufficient difference to ensure his profit.

Alam may not have intended to create a profitable business; it is just as likely that the willingness to pay over the odds arose from his neighbours' bidding up the price of his limited stock. And if people were willing to pay for it, who is to say that the convenience of buying from him did not, in fact, add value to his customers' purchases? The problem is that "convenience" does not have a ready equivalent in terms of work. It feels as if it should, but that very feeling obscures the connection between the value of something and the work giving rise to it, since the value of convenience is not underpinned with any associated work. When growing grain, or felling and sawing timber, there is a simple correlation between work and product; but in Alam's case he is able to make a profit without increasing the total amount of his work at all.

The work that pays Alam his profit is not his own, therefore, but that of his customers, who must now work harder than they otherwise would to earn the extra that they pay him. Here is a transfer of wealth from one to another in exchange for something that only has the perception of value. Alam's customers and neighbours have given up control over the value of their work in exchange for "convenience" in trading, which is exactly how transactional costs arise. To see how this works, consider the alternative. If Alam's neighbours pool their resources they can import a good quantity of timber, then draw from it as it suits them at no extra cost. Collaboration in this way produces free benefits, and these remain free for so long as the collaboration continues. Transactional costs however, can increase very rapidly. Carry on down the path that Alam has opened up and it will not be long before he controls the whole market and all its works. Once the market takes over, the connection between the price of something and the work that actually went into it will be lost forever.

Collaboration produces free benefits, and yet human nature is balanced on a knife edge that separates those benefits from the fear of being exploited when "joining in". Experimental studies show that people are far more concerned at losing out on what they have than they are at passing up on a potential gain. If they sense that others are "taking advantage" by not pulling their weight in a collaborative task they experience this as a loss to themselves. The disincentive this creates to participate easily outweighs in their minds the enormous gains to be had from free, collaborative working. For the much smaller number of people for whom losing out is an acceptable risk in the face of a potential gain, this creates a valuable opportunity. These are entrepreneurial types, whose willingness to embrace risk enables them to harness (and profit from) the labour of the risk-averse majority.

This relationship between entrepreneurs and the risk-averse leads directly to the creation of a market in labour, allowing wage levels to be established at a "going rate". The market economy is the antithesis to collaborative working; although it provides a mechanism for workers to discount the risk of being underpaid relative to one another, it does so at significant cost, since all of them now earn less than could be had through effective collaboration. Collaboration minimises transactional costs, but the market encourages them and the opportunities they create for turning a profit. So, although markets are associated with efficiency, this assumes that their purpose is to set the value of labour at the lowest sustainable level in order to maximise profits. If, however, the purpose of work is to keep people alive, warm, healthy and capable of leading flourishing lives, an efficient mechanism would be one that set the value of labour at the *highest* sustainable level, so that as much as possible of the wealth produced came back to the productive worker. To achieve this, an economy should be structured not to exploit people's fears of losing out but to remove those fears completely.

Today, people searching the market for the "best deal" from a range of intermediate suppliers are rarely more than dimly aware of the actual producers of the goods that they seek. The market has closed down the possibility of a direct relationship between consumer and producer, so the "best deal" that the market offers is really only the best of a number of deals all of which are poorer than could be achieved if producers and consumers were to collaborate directly in seeking to meet their shared aspirations. The problem that markets seek to solve, therefore, is really one of their own creation: in exploiting human weakness they create transactional barriers between producers and users, then usurp to themselves a highly profitable monopoly in the economic intermediation needed to negotiate those barriers. Their questionable achievement is to have normalised acquisitive behaviour in the face of a collaborative alternative from which, collectively, everyone would gain.

TO PROVIDE A contemporary context, consider the following. Since the drive for privatisation in the 1980s, Britain has pioneered a global fashion for outsourcing public services to competitive, profit-making businesses. Health, education, social services and the criminal justice system have all been drawn in; ideologically it is assumed that private enterprise is necessarily cheaper and more efficient than the public sector, since the profit motive keeps it sharp. The underlying objective, however, to engage private and commercial capital in the public realm, takes little account of the fact that the government can almost invariably borrow at a lower rate of return than that required by commercial finance.

With investment finance more expensive, the opportunities for a commercial provider to reduce the cost of services are limited. Either the quality of the service must diminish, or the work contained in it must be reduced or devalued. Generally it is a bit of both: the pressures of the profit-driven model have tended towards a more formulaic, less personalised approach to the delivery of services, as well as a deterioration in the number, pay and conditions of the employees providing them. One consequence, therefore, is a net transfer of wealth from these employees to taxpayers, upon whom lower taxes may now be levied since the services are cheaper. Considering that lower taxes favour the better off and that the profits taken by commercial service providers also gravitate towards people who have surplus wealth to invest, outsourcing increases the wealth gap through a further transfer of resources from the poor to the rich.

Poorer people on average make greater demands upon public education, health and social services, as well as imposing a greater burden upon the criminal justice system, so any further transfer of wealth from the poor to the rich tends towards an increase in the need for these services. Any saving to the public purse may, therefore, be illusory in the longer term, although the increase in the misery and consequences of human poverty is cumulative and decidedly real. At the same time the much vaunted consumer "choice", claimed as one of the key advantages of the market model in public services, is an authentic benefit only when there is true variety of provision. True variety is always more expensive, so the perception of choice is also often an illusion. Nowhere is this more evident than in the parody of choice associated with the markets for utility services such as telephony, electricity and gas.

In these markets, a fixed number of customers consumes a fixed quantity of indistinguishable and readily-available product, while a large number of suppliers seek to acquire them as customers by prevailing upon them to exercise their consumer choice. Since no new customers and no new economic activity are created, this "competition" is merely an extravagant exercise whereby the suppliers share out the customers between them. The government's response has been the creation of an infrastructure of regulatory bodies with formulaic names like Ofcom, Ofgem, Ofwat, etc., each custodian to a lengthy and complicated rulebook intended to ensure that some semblance of competition is kept alive. To what extent they may have succeeded is not really the point; all this effort to create an impression of a free market model has added several superfluous layers of transactional activity, the most egregious of which is the persistent and opaque marketing and sales activity to which the long-suffering public is routinely subjected.

The cost of this spurious competition, and the cost of servicing the bodies required to bring some semblance of regulation to it, is borne, naturally, by the users of these basic services. Similar costs abound among commercial providers of government-funded services, for whom the work of bidding for and managing a contract for profit must be shadowed by a government department or agency. The government selects the contractor, supervises and quality-assures it, takes responsibility for complaints against it, deals with any fall-out and hopes that whatever level of profit the contractor achieves can still be presented as "value for money". The whole edifice of out-sourcing and privatisation is riddled with duplication of effort and unintended costs. It is the irrational outcome of a series of apparently rational decisions, starting with the innocent intention of slimming down a bloated government bureaucracy and ending up creating a bogus market. Even wholesale intervention by the government cannot prevent this market from being rigged.

The outsourcing of public services to the private sector creates opportunities for corruption, profiteering, mis-selling and the exploitation of labour; but credit must also be given for that innocent intention – the desire to improve, through exposure to the market, the quality and affordability of services widely felt to have declined in the hands of bureaucratic state monopolies. The tension between these two starting-points flows from the marriage between profit-driven capitalism and social democracy that arose as a consequence of the post-war settlement. A service for the public benefit is, by definition, a social good, and cannot, therefore, be characterised as a cost of doing business; but the right of private investors to protect and increase their financial return is deeply embedded in market principles.

This difficulty is a recent one. Although the development of agriculture thousands of years ago created the surplus wealth that is the basis of capitalism, access to that wealth has, for most of history, flowed from the patronage of the state and its sovereign institutions. How this came about, and how it ended, is the subject of the next chapter.

Chapter 3

THE GILDED MONUMENTS OF PRINCES

From sovereign power to personal wealth over 6000 years

IN THE TIME before farming, a hunter called Mo went out to check his traps, and found that he had caught a gazelle. He killed the animal, heaved it onto his back and took it to his village. He knew that the meat would start to decay before he and his family could eat it all, but he did not waste time wondering what to do with the surplus. He kept what he could use, and gave the rest away to his neighbours.

Barter was no good. Mo couldn't barter with someone who had enough food already, nor with someone who had nothing to offer in return. It was either give it away or let it rot. To do the latter would be to let slip a material advantage, the advantage of strengthening the interdependent social group. For Mo, therefore, giving was a perfectly rational and self-interested act. It meant that something that he did not need could be used to make other people stronger. By keeping the group strong there was a better chance that they would continue to hunt successfully and be able to help him, should he need it. When producing life's essentials is difficult, the imperative is to waste as little as possible. A gift economy is the least wasteful system of distribution, an example of collaboration of the highest order in which wealth is passed on until it finds where it is most needed.

Many generations later came Alam, the world's first builders merchant, whom we met in Chapter 2. By then the plain where Mo had hunted was criss-crossed with irrigation ditches from the nearby river, and a thriving farming community was putting more grain in store than it could ever use. The opportunity to trade grain for timber with forest people who were short on winter food allowed both communities to prosper, turning their surplus capacity into something that brought a material improvement to their lives. Here, however, was not merely a solution to a problem but the start of a new process. Once "surplus" became convertible into "useful" the concept of needfulness appeared in a new light. There was no longer such a thing as "enough", meaning the amount that a person needs. There was still a minimum, but no decisive maximum, so Mo's concept of generous self-interest had much less traction. With this change, humanity had reached a decisive fork in the road, where one sign pointed to "need" and the other to "ownership" as the arbiter of entitlement to the fruits of wellbeing. The road to civilisation lay firmly on the latter path, with concepts such as employment, transactional profit and competitive advantage as milestones on the way.

To track the wealth in the world from this moment, it is necessary only to follow the builders. The decisive moment came nearly six thousand years ago, in the fertile region of Mesopotamia in modern Iraq, as the world's first cities came into being. They evolved in response to developments in farming, trading and social organisation, which created wealth surpluses so great that they could no longer be absorbed by the communities that produced them. Managing that wealth, and the issues of property rights, debt, security, employment, contract and investment that came with it, required a complex legal and administrative framework. Here was a call upon government that emphasised the role of authority in the social order and forged a strong connection between political power and material prosperity. Cities were not, therefore, merely big concentrations of people, but a new form of political and social organisation based upon the management and consumption of large surpluses of productive wealth.

Cities are home to the cives, the citizens for whom civilisation is named. Among these are merchants, law-makers, administrators and soldiers, whose function is to channel surplus wealth into the city and to maintain the social and economic framework within which it is consumed. Making use of the wealth, while adding their own work to it, are the architects, engineers, painters, sculptors and skilled crafts-people who create and ornament the civic environment, and the priests, poets, musicians and entertainers who provide the religious, social and cultural activity that give that environment its meaning. The architecture that makes a city is institutional in scale and purpose. The capacity to construct such buildings and the political, religious and cultural status they represent all reflect the amount of surplus wealth that a civilisation has at its disposal. Its transformative effect can be seen by comparing two construction projects, both commenced at about the same time in the third millennium B.C. One is the necropolis at Giza, in Egypt, dominated by the great pyramid of Khufu; the other is Stonehenge, on Salisbury Plain in England.

Egypt in the Old Kingdom was a civilisation in the true sense, with surplus wealth so great that the construction of the Giza pyramids took place over three generations of a single ruling family in little more than a hundred years. The god-like status of the royal family imbued the project with a clear purpose: the fertility of the Nile valley derived from the annual flooding, part of the rhythm of the seasons which the gods were believed to hold in their gift. The successful transition of the mortal king to the afterlife could therefore be characterised as a social and economic – as wells as religious – imperative. The construction itself has been likened to the space programme[1] – a hugely expensive public project designed to stimulate the economy and keep people in work, all directed towards a great "national" achievement. Rapid advances were made in the arts and sciences, in astronomy, mathematics, surveying, transport and construction techniques, and above all in the organisational capacity required to bring all these elements into play. A sophisticated system of taxation and record-keeping kept the wealth flowing upwards through the economy from the 90% or so of the population who worked on the land.

Stonehenge is different. It was not the product of a single inspiration but evolved in stages over two thousand years. Although the monument itself is evidence of a successful, cohesive and technically sophisticated society, the enormous productive surpluses nec-

---

1   Lehner, M. *The Complete Pyramids*, Thames & Hudson, London, 1997

essary for city life were lacking and this neolithic culture did not develop as a civilisation in the true sense. One can picture a people stretched to the very limit of their economic and technical resources, gradually developing the ceremonial landscape of which Stonehenge is the centrepiece.

Stonehenge was a place of pilgrimage, to which people came to observe religious rites or to access mystical and healing powers. As such, it has the character of a collaborative social endeavour quite distinct from the uncompromising statement of ownership and individual prestige that the pyramids embody. Building the pyramids was collaborative only in the sense that lots of people took part. They speak of the capacity to control surplus wealth absolutely, a capacity dependent upon social stratification and occupational differentiation, an institutionalised "class" system that is one of the characteristics that civilisation brings. Those early Pharaohs had near absolute power, and the religious awe in which they were held was backed by a political, administrative and religious hierarchy – an aristocracy of landowners and priesthood all beholden to the king for their positions, wealth and status. Inequality, therefore, was hardwired into civilisation from the earliest time.

FAST FORWARD NEARLY four thousand years, and William of Normandy, fresh from his success in the Battle of Hastings, found himself with the entire land and wealth of England at his disposal. The principle upon which this authority rested was essentially no different to that which empowered King Khufu to build his Great Pyramid. It is that of sovereignty, or the power of the state legitimised in its sovereign person or body. Control of land is the evidence of this, since sovereign power extends both to its allocation and the right to share in its production. William's approach was much like Khufu's, too; he distributed land to his followers, who held it subject to his power and distributed it further among their own followers in return for military, religious and other services. This pattern of land tenure meant that control of wealth-production was closely interwoven with the social, religious and political fabric.

The Normans were prodigious builders. Five hundred castles were constructed in the twenty years that followed the Conquest. Most, initially, were earth and timber, but imposing stone towers were built in key locations and many others were re-built in stone in the subsequent century. Here was the physical evidence of the sovereignty that William exercised over the land; meanwhile an even more ambitious programme of ecclesiastical building spoke for a parallel claim to sovereignty over the destiny of the human soul. That claim rested ultimately with the Christian pope as the representative of God on earth, who competed effectively with the temporal power of kings, princes and emperors. As in England, so across much of Europe, cathedrals, monasteries and churches sprung up everywhere between the 11th and the 14th centuries as the vast wealth of the mediaeval church gave rise to an architectural achievement to rival even the monumental structures of the Egyptian dynasties. Europe's great abbeys and cathedrals stand firmly in the same tradition as the pyramids at Giza, their very existence giving legitimacy to the social and religious order that created them, while simultaneously placing both wealth and political power in the hands of a powerful elite.

From the birth of civilisation until at least the 17th century in Europe, distinctions of wealth, power and social status were sustained by the twin pillars of religion – with its key to life beyond the grave – and the sovereign control of land. The connection between religion and the sovereignty of kings was not as close in mediaeval Europe as it was under the Pharaohs, but it was close enough. Monarchs invoked divine right to establish their legitimacy. Religion underpinned the sovereignty that gave them power over land, which they exercised through the confiscation and granting of estates. The most dramatic fusion of these principles occurred in late medieval England, when Henry VIII dissolved the monasteries, appropriated their colossal land holdings and declared himself head of the English church.

Henry's historic act presaged a turning point, since the landed wealth that he took from the church soon found its way, by gift or purchase, into the hands of the secular aristocracy. The English Civil War, which culminated in the execution of a king, demonstrated the fallibility of monarchy and the willingness of the landed class to assert an independent power. The replacement of feudal service with money rents, and an accelerating process of land enclosure designed to create more productive and profitable holdings, brought new opportunities for land entrepreneurship, so that estate management increasingly reflected rights of private ownership rather than the sovereign weal. Following the restoration of monarchy under Charles II an act of parliament finally abolished the residual feudal dues to which the crown was entitled, replacing the lost income with taxes on consumables such as alcohol and tea.

Here, in England, at least, was the final, symbolic rupture with a principle of land ownership that would have been recognisable in Egypt some five thousand years earlier. Despite the polite fiction that land in England continues to be held "in fee simple" (i.e. "of the crown"), during the 17th century it was firmly established as the prime measure of inalienable personal wealth. It is a change that was reflected dramatically in architecture. For whereas, previously, great buildings had mostly been dedicated to religion or were connected to the political or military aspects of government, now individual wealth asserted itself, and money was poured into the construction of private houses, the purpose of which was to establish the status of the independently rich.

RENAISSANCE ITALY WAS the forerunner. The Renaissance took off because rich patrons wished to make an architectural statement of their private wealth, and they filled their new buildings with magnificent works of art to emphasise their cultural and social credentials. The movement commenced in Florence in the 1440s, where bankers and merchants vied with each other in the construction of private palaces in the newly fashionable classical style. It spread rapidly across Europe, its path eased by the wealth flowing from the new avenues of trade and plunder then opening up towards the Americas and the Far East. Nowhere was it more enthusiastically taken up than in Britain where, between the 16th and the 19th centuries, many thousand significant country houses were built.

That coy phrase "country house" is highly misleading, since it encompasses a body of sumptuous palace architecture that runs from Longleat, commenced in 1567, to Castle Drogo, completed in 1930, and takes in, among many others, Chatsworth, Blenheim, Kedleston, Woburn and Stowe. The concentration of wealth among British landowners over nearly four centuries gave rise to artistic patronage on a truly heroic scale, combining lavish architecture and interior decoration with a wholly innovative approach to landscape design and the acquisition of priceless collections of books, antiquities, objet d'art, sculpture and paintings. Taken collectively, Britain's country mansions, the landscapes created for them and the collections they house represent a unique cultural phenomenon – an achievement of wealth and connoisseurship unrivalled in history.

Like the Pharaohs of ancient Egypt and the church of medieval Europe, it was the capacity of landowners to appropriate the wealth generated by the people who worked the land that made this achievement possible. But, unlike the pyramids and the great cathedrals, the country houses of Britain aspired to no public purpose beyond the maintenance of a social hierarchy. Land remained the backbone of the social order in Britain until well into the 19th century, as any reader of Jane Austen, George Eliot or Anthony Trollope knows. In a society where the measure of gentility was to live well without the appearance of work, the ownership of land was the best evidence and guarantee. Since "class" had, as today, more to do with education and wealth than with genetics, a transformation from trade to gentility in a single generation was perfectly feasible when sealed through the purchase of a landed estate.

The status of land was connected both with its permanence and the position it afforded in the social structure of the countryside, itself a hangover from a feudal past. Until the mid-19th century, however, it was the primary source, as well as *prima facie* evidence, of wealth, and as such its significance went beyond social status to that of a business in its own right. It was also a source of capital: the link between land and the wealth derived from manufacturing and trade became closer as industrialisation took hold and international markets became more accessible. While successful entrepreneurs bought land to assert their respectability, established landowners leveraged their assets both to increase productivity and to fund commercial activities elsewhere.

With this in mind, the enclosure of common land (including the Highland clearances in Scotland) advanced apace. Whereas, in the 16th century, the Tudor monarchs had sought to protect village-based livelihoods by restricting enclosure for sheep farming, by the 18th century the power of the landowners was such that the process could accelerate, encouraged still further by agricultural innovations that permitted large scale, more efficient use of the land. The agricultural revolution not only changed the rural economy but paved the way for the world's first industrial society, in which a combination of technological innovation, ready capital, a workforce increasingly separated from the land and rising access to world markets provided the conditions for mechanised factory production on a large scale.

For thousands of years, most people lived, worked and died producing food from the land. It was not a life choice or a job offer; it was the reality of the human condition. Then, in little more than a century of sustained innovation – in science and technology, finance, transport, social organisation, management, politics and trade – all of that changed forever in a way that has touched the entire globe. The rapid acceleration in productivity brought about by the agricultural and industrial innovations that began in Britain in the 18th century is arguably the most important development in human history since the dawn of civilisation. Civilisation itself – with its capacity for political and social organisation based upon the management and consumption of surplus wealth – is the six thousand year old innovation that made it possible, but it took most of those six thousand years for a form of social organisation to emerge with the qualities to catalyse this tremendous advance.

That form is a new paradigm of civilisation – a fundamental change in the social contract that had sustained civilisation since its earliest times. The sovereignty of the god-appointed monarch – in whose person reposed the interests of the people, for better or for worse – was replaced by a new sovereignty, residing in the individual and rooted in the right of private ownership and the freedom to act out of personal self-interest. Far from being a mass movement, this change started among a small group of the already-wealthy. In detaching themselves from their obligations to monarchy and the sovereign realm, they successfully re-defined the relationships that bound society, leading rapidly to individualisation at every social level. For the great majority, freedom from their shackles to the land also separated them from the subsistence that the land provided. Henceforward they would take their chances in a world in which anyone, theoretically, might prosper on their own account, but the many who did not would be vulnerable to a degree of exploitation no less insidious, profound and degenerative than the conditions that they left behind.

THAT IS NOT how history has chosen to be written. It is far more impressive to envisage the private wealth of Britain's landowners as a collective declaration of independence from the divine rights of monarchy, their display of connoisseurship merely one facet of an intellectual and political enlightenment that would lead, eventually, to the Universal Declaration of Human Rights. This celebrated narrative is played out through the development of constitutional monarchy and parliamentary democracy, the creation and dismantling of a global empire, and victory in a succession of "wars of liberation" against totalitarian or reactionary oppressors, from Louis XIV of France to, most recently, Colonel Gaddafi of Libya. Running parallel, however, is a darker narrative, of the creation of a global economic system designed to concentrate wealth at certain key points of interconnection, and in the hands of an elite even more powerful than the landed aristocracy that it has quietly supplanted.

London is the paradigm, replicated now in many commercial centres across the globe, all acquiring disproportionate prosperity through their control of the flow of economic activity. The halls of business where this takes place are the true successors to those elegant mansions and their vast estates. The grand architectural statements of the later 20th and the 21st centuries are not the products either of private patronage or the sovereign state but the imposing towers and massive glass, concrete and marble blocks that house the offices and headquarters of trans-national commerce. This commerce is now so wealthy and pervasive that it has assumed for itself the trappings of sovereign power.

As Castle Drogo – the last great architectural gasp of an aspirant land-owning class – was struggling into existence in the 1920s, its architect, Sir Edwin Lutyens, was already venturing into this brave new world, constructing in the City of London a vast new headquarters for the Anglo-Persian Oil Company (now BP and still one of the largest companies in the world). The city's historic fabric restricted high-rise development until the post-war boom of the 1950s, so the favoured approach was a palazzo form in an extravagant, neo-Baroque / Art Deco fusion, a contemporary reinterpretation of the grandeur and formalism of the early period of country house building. These style cues were carried over the Atlantic, re-expressed there in vertical form as the business powerhouses of New York, Chicago and elsewhere vied with one another to build the tallest, grandest temples to the new commercial dawn. Best known is The Empire State Building (1931), famous for forty years as the world's tallest, and a cultural icon for the American dream. There is a certain irony in that: it was build speculatively to provide office space to rent and stood half empty for many years. It heralded, nonetheless, the emergence of office building as the characteristic architectural form of the modern age.

Across the globe, the skylines of cities have been transformed by this building revolution. The demand for office space and commercial centres has seen an explosion of construction, both high-rise and low, most recently and dramatically in the new commercial centres of Asia and the Middle East. In a mature economy such as Britain's the figures speak for themselves: between 1974 and 2008 the amount of office space per head of population much more than doubled to accommodate a similar increase in the number of people employed in desk-bound activities[1]. Several tall, landmark buildings arose in

---

1   In the same period the amount of space given over to shopping and warehousing rose by 50%. Factories and industrial units, on the other hand, declined by 15%. Source: Office of National Statistics.

London in the 1960s and '70s, including the once-iconic Post Office Tower (1962); but it was only when that tower was surpassed by the National Westminster Tower[1] in 1980 that skyscraper fever really caught hold. Now, the public is familiar with the *Gherkin*[2], Heron Tower (currently the tallest in the City of London), the *Shard* (the tallest building in Europe), the *Walkie-Talkie*, the Pinnacle and the *Cheese Grater*[3], all high rise constructions of distinctive design that demonstrate how offices have become the trophy buildings of the investment world.

In total, there are approximately a hundred million square metres of office space in England, enough for about eight million people – well over a quarter of the working population – to work. What do they do all day, and why is there so much more of it to do (more than twice as much) than there was thirty years ago? The answer lies in the enormous increase in transactional activity within the economy, which has allowed it to grow so fast. These employees are working away on behalf of those who control the surplus in the economy, just as people once worked on on royal, state and religious projects and the private projects of the independently rich. The difference is that those projects involved spending on consumption: payments to the craftsmen and artists who built and decorated a country house, or to a footman in a powdered wig to stand behind the chair of its owner at dinner, were extravagant instances of discretionary spending. In a modern, office-based economy, the object of employers is not to consume wealth but to accumulate more of it through the transactional activities of those they employ.

FROM THE BIRTH of civilisation right through to 18th century Europe and beyond, most people were primary wealth producers, bound to a sovereign power or social elite which controlled the wealth that was surplus to people's basic needs. In the past fifty years, however, in developed economies, the number of primary producers has

1   25 Old Broad Street, later re-branded *Tower 42*
2   30 St Mary Axe, formerly known as the Swiss Re building
3   20 Fenchurch Street, Bishopsgate Tower and the Leadenhall Building, respectively

dropped rapidly, so that now the incomes of a majority of working people have become a transactional cost on that smaller number of producers of real wealth. Office buildings and shopping centres are the monuments to this new order. They are greater in size and number, and they absorb surplus wealth even more effectively, than the temples, mausoleums, palaces, cathedrals, castles and great houses of earlier epochs.

Whether they are capable of inspiring the same degree of awe, and whether, once in ruins, future generations will gaze upon them and wonder at such marvels of human endeavour, it is too early to say. The more immediate task is to try to explain why they have come into being in the first place.

Chapter 4

INSTITUTIONAL GAIN

How the corporate economy puts profit before useful work

WHO BUILDS, OWNS and occupies the new commercial palaces, the office buildings and shopping centres that dominate the skylines of the world's cities? Not the kings, bishops and aristocratic landowners of earlier centuries, that is for sure. In most cases the owners of all this conspicuous construction are not even people at all, in the human sense, but an inanimate form of being, a legal fiction conjured up by an act of parliament and existing only in the eyes of the law. These legal persons are commercial companies, in which the wealth of many individual people is combined anonymously. They rose to prominence in Britain in the later 19th century following the Joint Stock Companies Act of 1844. Before long, almost all business of any size was conducted within these new, impersonal frameworks.

The introduction of a general right to form a company was the clearest possible indication that the source of sovereignty was no longer to be found in the divine right of kings. Hitherto, incorporation had been a jealously guarded gift of the sovereign power. In the middle ages it was limited to civic and religious organisations, to provide a legal framework for their existence beyond the mortal lives of individual members. There was little call for commercial companies until the world opened up in the 15th century, when merchants sought a means to spread the risks of international trade. Control of this trade into and out of Europe rested with sovereign powers as part of the "mercantilist" system, which saw trade as an arm of national policy. Trading companies could only be established by Royal Charter with the purpose of extending national power. Among the first and greatest of these was the British East India Company, granted a charter by Elizabeth I in 1600.

By the time of the 1844 Companies Act, mercantilism had long been in retreat, the national interest either replaced by or subsumed into the private interests of merchants and traders. Many of these were now members of the governing class, so the promotion of business opportunities through the regulation of the competing financial interests of investors, managers and creditors was a political as well as a commercial imperative. The thrust of the legislation was the protection from bad or fraudulent management of an individual's accumulated wealth when deployed as capital. All companies had to be incorporated and registered, and the rights and responsibilities of shareholders and directors were clearly set out. In 1855 the Limited Liability Act took the process a stage further, allowing shareholders to escape liability for the debts of a company beyond the nominal value of their shares.

The rise of incorporation followed closely on the heels of industrialisation, and it is the succession of these two developments that has permitted the colossal increase in economic activity since that time. Early industrialists were focused on production, particularly of goods that could be sold or exchanged in profitable overseas markets. The idea that further wealth could be accumulated through the use of money as capital rather than through working was, however, of interest to anybody who had funds to invest. The gentlefolk with whom Jane Austen peopled her pages had limited options in this respect. Those without landed estates kept their money in government bonds, offering safe but moderate returns of three or five per cent but with no prospect of capital accumulation. Investing money in speculative projects was considered rash, not least because the social consequences of losing even a modest income were so severe.

Incorporation, particularly after the introduction of limited liability, changed this by providing a relatively safe route to diversification of investment and the potential for a higher return. It brought large amounts of capital into business, but in doing so it transformed commercial investment from an entrepreneurial to a rentier activity:

people committing money, time and effort at their own risk were increasingly replaced by people knowing little of the activity they invested in and wanting only a reliable financial return. Maximising this return, rather than the productive and creative aspects of commerce, became the over-riding consideration in the regulated business model that incorporation ushered in.

Just as great architecture through the ages has reflected the locus of power, office buildings have become the predominant architecture of the modern age because they are where corporate power resides. Imposing tower blocks and company headquarters are the most visible symbols of this concentration of wealth, but offices and shopping centres characterise the corporate economy much more profoundly through their function than their appearance. If 5% of the work paid for in the price of a pair of trainers takes place in a factory, most of the rest takes place in offices and shops. This explains why the surplus wealth once poured into religious buildings, castles and great country houses is now directed in even greater amounts to the construction of such buildings. Offices and shops are the places where transactional activities are carried out, and if £5 can be turned into £100 through this sort of work, it is no wonder that investors have built on such a grand scale.

INCORPORATION IS THE *summum bonum* of the transactional commercial world. Its genius lies in having a single, consistent objective – the pursuit of profit – from which all other considerations are either subtly or explicitly excluded. Whereas, before incorporation, the good or evil that flowed from controlling the sources of wealth was a question of human character – the qualities that distinguished a tyrant from a just monarch, a negligent from a concerned landlord or a greedy mill owner from a caring employer – the capital that is invested in a company is not burdened with moral responsibility for the way it behaves.

As a framework for conducting business, incorporation overcomes the challenges posed by the infinite variety of human behaviour. Individuals are rarely consistent; they are responsive to human relationships and emotion, are unpredictable in their reactions and have multiple, complex and varying motivations. They may seek wealth, or excitement, or security, or friendship, or have the desire to innovate or do something worthwhile, or any combination of these or others. When they work for companies, however, individuals are expected to suppress these natural behavioural traits or direct them towards the company's interests. They may act neither according to their personal whim nor their private principles, but must do what is judged most likely to increase the shareholders' financial return. The directors of a company, in particular, have a legal obligation to perform in this way, for which reason the connections they cause the company to make (with customers, suppliers, employees, etc.) are not true relationships, but contingent arrangements intended to secure maximum financial gain.

Once, a king who exploited his subjects to his own profit was called a bad king; now, a company that exploits its employees, customer and suppliers to the profit of its shareholders is called a successful company, the measure of which is to be seen in the prices on the stock exchange. In a competition between these "legal persons" and the living, breathing people whom the law calls "natural persons", companies have many advantages. Most importantly, they are not "needy" in the human sense. Every real human being is both part producer and part consumer of what is needed. Consumption by humans – whether of food, material wealth or human wellbeing – is central to the purpose of production, which is to sustain human life. Companies are legal creations that do not "live" and need not consume anything for its own sake. They are only intermediate consumers, which means that they take in only the ingredients of their own commercial output.

Lacking inherent wants or needs of their own, and having no true personality or character, companies have no affinity with the needs of others, either. No real person is immune to cold, or illness, or the eventuality of death, so their determination to accumulate wealth is moderated by a context and perspective in a socially engaging world. Even the richest real person can imagine what it is like to starve, and even the richest real person will one day die, at which point their wealth will pass to other people who may apply it in a completely different way. Companies, however, go on forever, their behaviour dictated by memoranda and articles of association that, devoid of human inconsistencies, enable them to approach decision-making in unvarying, process-driven terms. They are the "ideal person" of the classical economist: they always behave rationally and in their own self-interest (as they see it), as they are required to do by the framework of law that gives them their being.

The canal-building Duke of Bridgewater was personally liable for the expense and risk of everything that he created. This is one reason why, as the richest person in Britain at the end of the 18th century, he was so much less rich in real terms than the richest people today. Today's super-rich have leveraged the wealth of other investors through incorporation, which enables their own wealth to accumulate at a rate otherwise disproportionate to the amount of money they started out with, and at minimal risk. Company directors often own shares in the companies they manage, in which case they speak for and direct their own wealth, as well as that of others. But they do so in a context that allows them to separate their human selves from the moral consequences of their corporate decisions. Ultimately, the maintenance of shareholder value – the measure of the willingness of the wealthy to participate in the company's activity by purchasing its shares – is the only barrier between company directors and a largely unaccountable power (including the power to remunerate themselves generously). That power can be enormous – the largest five hundred companies in the world by market capitalisation were collectively worth US$3,600 for every member of the human race in 2012 – but each is directed typically by a handful of people. The scale of transactions of which such companies are capable place them on a par with independent nation states as a measure of their power to dictate the lives and destiny of those who come within their orbit.

BECAUSE REAL PEOPLE have real, basic needs, they must seek to make a return *in the moment* on the limited amount of work that they can physically do. They need food and shelter today, not the prospect of them at some indeterminate point in the future. Their wealth, therefore, is measured largely by their capacity to meet immediate wants and needs. They may be able to borrow, but this merely creates an additional cost, both in interest and a charge against uncertain future earnings.

A company, on the other hand, is measured largely on the basis of its future potential. The difference is seen in the working of financial markets compared with conventional markets that supply human needs in real time. In the latter case, people buy fruit and vegetables to eat today, or in the next few days, using the money that currently have and at a price that reflects the immediate value to them of the food that they choose. Markets that trade in financial instruments such as company shares are dealing in predictions of profits to come in the future. Such "future promise" has value in its own right, independently of current profits, and the price payable for the shares reflects the value of this promise rather than any immediate return. If investors think that the profits are going to rise at some point, the value of the shares rises now, in anticipation of that golden future.

It follows that there are two ways of making money out of owning shares. One is to pocket the dividend that the company pays out as a share in its profits. The higher the dividend relative to the price of the share, the better is the percentage return. The other is to sell the shares for a higher price than was paid for them. In this case, the higher the price of the share relative to the dividend, the better the shareholder is likely to do. Most shareholders are looking to make money in both ways, and it is the tension between the two that drives public companies, the shares of which are easily traded. On the one hand, they need to ensure their future prospects, to keep the share price rising and enable shareholders to achieve a capital gain; on the other, they need to ensure that profitability (or the expectation of profitability) keeps up with the rising share price, so that shareholders achieve an acceptable dividend. As a share price rises, therefore, both its actual and promise value have to work ever harder to sustain it at the higher levels.

This perpetual tension between rising shareholder expectations and actual profitability means that a company that wishes to "succeed" in the terms of the market may never stand still but must constantly seek out ways to increase the scale of its activity. Real growth, based on actual demand, is limited by the physical capacity of people to make things and their need and willingness to consume them. Sometimes the demand for a product does explode – the number of mobile telephone handsets that are bought and replaced annually is beyond human reason – but even in this market there are winners and losers, and for a company to rely simply upon making more of the same will not generally give rise to the sustained increases in profits and share price that its shareholders seek.

In the real economy, people grow or make things that other people want. They have limited exposure to economic risk because their work results in products that have inherent and acknowledged value. In the pre-industrial economy, when many things were made to order, this risk was particularly low, but there was much less opportunity to make excessive profits. That opportunity came with long-distance trade, when, at a time of slow, expensive and uncertain transport, with a high risk of shipwreck and loss, the value to be added from the relocation of goods over long distances was commensurately high. Items of relatively low value in one place could be sold for much more in another, and the difference between the two on each leg of a trading journey was great enough to cover both the considerable costs and the risk of failure, while still yielding a handsome profit.

The sheer scale of that difference is evidenced by the extraordinary cost burdens that traders were willing to undertake. From the 16th to the 19th century, the Portuguese, Dutch and British trading companies to the Far East built far-flung networks of fortifications and trading posts, maintained large fleets of naval as well as merchant vessels, raised armies and carried out extensive military operations, all out of the proceeds of their commercial and trading activities. The profits of buying in one market and selling in another vastly exceeded the money to be made out of mere manufacture, although the scale both of the investments and the risks meant that those able to share these burdens through participation in a company were much more likely to thrive.

The comparative simplicity of global transport and the regulation of international trade in the modern age means that companies today are denied the excessive profits to be gained from remoteness and the rare and exotic, but must seek new ways of creating equivalent opportunities. The underlying principle has not changed that much, as we have already seen: if a pair of shoes produced in south east Asia for £3 can sell on a British high street for £80 or more, that would not have been bad going, even for a 16th century adventurer. The difference, however, and the risks associated with it, derive no longer from the distance or difficulty of the journey, but from a series of branding, advertising and other transactional processes applied to the goods once they arrive. When product is plentiful, the success or failure of the company relies upon the added value of market place-ment. Get this right, and the profits will surely flow.

No company exemplifies this more effectively that Apple, Inc., which in 2012 became the world's largest company by market capi-talisation, or the total value of its shares. Apple retains for itself the huge margins and commensurate profits once enjoyed by those trad-ers in exotic Eastern spices, and it does so on the basis of values derived from the intangibles of perception – social and cultural stand-ing, aesthetic taste and peer pressure – all of which are wrapped up in a notion of consumer desirability with which the 17th century spice traders would have been entirely familiar.

Like those spice traders, Apple deals in real products, but, also like them, its profits lie not in the products themselves, but what it does with them. It does not undertake the low risk, low margin activity of employing people to make what it designs and sells. The price of the inputs and the market value of labour are too easily established to give any one producer a significant marginal advantage in that game. It does seek to add value through its cutting-edge design, but this alone is also insufficient, as the company's experience in the 1990s showed. Design, like any production characteristic, can be adopted by competitors, just as Apple's range of telephone, tablet and computer devices sits alongside an increasing number of rival products with similar functionality. Although its designs maintain some distinctiveness, Apple's stratospheric success as a company is due much less to the products themselves than to the transactional nexus that it has created around them.

Relative to its size, Apple is not a particularly large employer. It is, however, labour-intensive in one respect: half of its 84,000 staff in 2013 were working in its shops, of which there were 416 worldwide, generating annual sales of over $20 billion from about 425,000 square metres of retail space[1]. These figures place Apple in the top fifty of the world's largest retailers, and by far the most successful in terms of sales per square metre. What is more, its shop sales in 2013 were a mere 12% of its total; it has many other routes to market, including the mobile phone networks that distribute the majority of its handsets. Nonetheless, its shops play an important role in maintaining the relationships with customers that give Apple's products their desirability. The shops themselves are a highly successful exercise in product placement, some of which the company admits are "high-profile venues to promote brand awareness."

Apple's shops characterise highly visibly its place at the interface between the consumer and technology. Less visible, but arguably even more effective in controlling the transactional nexus, is the way that it mediates the content that its customers use on the devices that they purchase. In 2012 Apple's iTunes service was estimated to have a 64% share of the music download market, amounting to 29% of all retail music sales[2]. As well as 26 million items of music, Apple also had, by its own estimation, more than 700,000 applications, 190,000 TV episodes and 45,000 films available for purchase by download on to its devices. Although iTunes music and video may be accessed using rival software, the company's project of seamlessly integrating its hardware and software with the sale of online content under the Apple brand represents a masterclass in transactional advantage,

1   Data for Apple Inc. is from its 2013 annual report
2   Market research by NPD Group, widely reported

whereby the desirability of the devices themselves, and the media applications and download libraries that the company has optimised for their use, feed off one another in the retail market.

Both the hardware and the software are routes into the transaction, and both represent big profit-making opportunities for the company. The customer first pays heavily for the device, one of the chief design functions of which is to give them access to Apple's online catalogue, for which they subsequently also pay. Thus a retail electronics company has re-invented itself to manage and profit from the relationship between the creators and the consumers of musical, literary, cinematographic and other digitally distributable work. For the owner of an Apple device, its seamless integration with content services is the whole point of the purchase. Its users want Apple in their lives, a marketing achievement that illustrates the key role played by transactional interactions in the success of a modern corporate trader.

As the world's foremost music retailer and most profitable shopkeeper, Apple spends much more time and energy packaging, branding and selling both physical and downloadable products than it does creating them. Its research and development budget is a mere 3% of its admittedly colossal sales, whereas its selling, general and administrative costs are more than twice as much. In 2013 Apple spent $4.5 billion designing products, and a further $107 billion having them made to those designs by third party manufacturers, before selling them on for $171 billion, incurring $10 billion of marketing and sales expenses along the way. That is good business for Apple's shareholders, for whom the company earned $40 per share, but that $50 billion of marginal gain is a net cost to its customers, suppliers and staff.

APPLE HAS LEARNED how to leverage its transactional advantage in every possible way, and in doing so it is merely emulating what every successful company aspires to – shifting vast quantities of wealth upwards through the economy towards its already wealthy shareholders. In 2013 the company was sitting on $150 billion or so of cash assets, a sum that, if distributed judiciously among deprived communities, could bring life-changing benefits to millions of families. The love-in between Apple and its customer base should not, therefore, be permitted to obscure the essential truth, that the interests of companies and individuals in an economy are rarely the same.

For individuals, it is in their interests to collaborate to make the economy as productive as possible of real wealth. For companies, the size of the real economy is much less important that the profit they can extract from it. A company making 5% from an economic "cake" worth, say, £1 million earns £50,000. Were it to collaborate with others in doubling the size of the cake to £2 million, but see its profit reduced to 2% as a consequence, it would be worse off by £10,000. The cake in question is the real, usable wealth that an economy produces. An economy abundant with real wealth is good for people but does not necessarily help corporate growth, since abundance reduces the control that enables companies to increase their profits.

Once again, the mobile phone market illustrates the point. The world is awash with such devices, which do broadly similar things. There is, however, a big price range, with many inexpensive offerings, a smaller but significant number of high profile products at the expensive end and rather less in between. It is certainly possible for the industry to sell phones inexpensively, and it does so in large numbers. Possible, however, does not mean profitable: as with most things, including cars and dishwashers as well as electronic devices, the difference in the work required to produce a top-end compared with a low-end product does not justify the difference in price. With mobile phones varying from £0.99 to £700 on a "pay as you go" basis, it should be clear that top-end models are far more profitable for all concerned.

The only thing that really interests a company about their customers is what they can and are willing to afford. A customer who "underspends" is a lost opportunity, so cheaper offerings are made of a lower quality or performance than they need be, in order to justify the much higher prices at the top of the range. If the selling points of an expensive dishwasher are, for example, energy efficiency and quietness, it only works as a marketing strategy if the cheaper models are noisy and inefficient. The efficiency is largely a matter of how the machine's programmes are set up; the noise is generally a matter of better insulation. In both cases the marginal cost is likely to be tiny, but the price may vary by 50 or 100%.

All customers lose out in this situation: the poorer get noisy, inefficient machines, the richer get ripped off. The interests of real people (as opposed to "target markets") would best be served if all machines were as good as they could possibly be for a given price. Since, however, companies are dependent upon marginal gains, they have to give people plausible reasons to to pay for more than they want or need. Target marketing does just that: "three for two" offers in supermarkets sit at one end of this approach while over-expensive manufactured goods are at the other. At the other end of the mobile telephony market, far away from the producers of shiny devices, the companies that provide the signals and make the connections offered 7.5 million different tariffs to UK customers in 2012. Research[1] showed that, as a consequence of this market complexity, 40% of what people spent on mobile telephony could have been avoided had they been on the optimal tariff. The total wasted was nearly £6 billion, or £127 per user per year. The price of this enormous unearned profit to the companies is the transactional activity of designing, marketing, managing and maintaining all those millions of consumer options.

In a transactional economy, effective competition between companies reduces their profits, which inclines them to compete with one another as little as they can get away with. Opportunities for increased profit come from a much less equal competition, a tactical struggle in which companies seek to extract as much wealth as possible from their customers, only the most astute, persistent or vociferous of whom are likely to notch up even a marginal win. Governments have learned to tolerate and even welcome this reality, since it is the capacity of the corporate economy to leverage transactional activity into spectacular "geometric" growth that tells the world, at least on paper, how a country is doing.

1   *The billmonitor.com national mobile report 2012*

It is a chimerical growth, fuelled by cheap labour and ready credit. Apple is merely the most prominent exemplar, buying its products from companies that manufacture in the world's low pay labour markets and building its profile on the back of a retail operation in which low pay is also the norm. In the mobile phone market the credit flows so freely that customers are often not aware that they are making use of it. The service providers pay for the phones, and the customers repay them over many months in the blithe belief that it is really only the calls and services they use that are generating their monthly charge.

The availability of ready credit is one of many ways in which companies persuade people to transact with them, casually disrupting their capacity to create wealth for themselves. The self-supply of wealth that people naturally undertake embraces creative, physical, intellectual and relational activities that are highly productive of human wellbeing. People may sleep more, or sing, or write poetry, or walk, or talk, or spend more time with their family and friends, all of which are manifestations of the flourishing that true wealth permits. There are also many fields of work, such as caring for children and the elderly, housework, building, gardening and growing, cooking, dress-making and mending, all of which have the potential to contribute to human wellbeing, provided that people have the unpressurised time to do such things for themselves.

These activities are not measured as economic output unless commercial companies can intervene. Increasingly, they seek to do so: more "leisure" is now commercially supplied that at any other time in history, and people are encouraged to buy more and more of the things that they could do for themselves as a consequence of the pressure with which this commercial world embraces them. The long hours of work required to pay for these things leaves no time for the self-supply of wealth that does not arrive through a commercial intervention, and this is exactly how the corporate world, and the governments that collude with it, like things to be.

Chapter 5

PARADING THE EMPEROR'S NEW CLOTHES

Life in a transactional economy

A TRANSACTIONAL ECONOMY is one in which far more of the work people do is spent transacting (buying, selling, negotiating, managing, administering and checking) than is spent in producing real, usable wealth – the things that people want and need. Western economies are all like this, but the size of its financial services activity makes Britain an extreme case.

People living in a transactional economy enjoy, on average, less useful wealth than they ought to be able to gain from the amount of work that they do. They are working much longer hours than would be necessary if the economy did not generate so much transactional work, and the material gain that this generates is distributed very unevenly. The poorest people lack the essentials of life, and even the relatively poor (the much-discussed "squeezed middle" of economic demographics) may be pushed to meet their basic needs of food, clothing and shelter. Nor are the better-off unaffected: people not needing to count the cost of life's essentials also routinely experience a shortage of provision in other ways. You do not have to be the slightest bit poor to experience the diminution of quality of life represented by an under-resourced school, a pot-holed road, a lonely, neglected, elderly relative, a lengthy waiting-list for medical care, the non-availability of expensive drugs and procedures, or a lack of research into a life-threatening condition. Similarly, a dysfunctional, underfunded, criminal justice system may leave you feeling vulnerable, and you may work for so long every day that you are able to spend nowhere near enough time with your partner and children.

Good schools, smooth roads, generous, engaging care for the elderly, effective medicine and hospital care, a safe, humane, healthy environment and quality time with one's family: all these things, and many others, are valuable in themselves, bringing real benefits to the quality of life and helping people to flourish. They are not more important than food, clothing and shelter, but they serve as a reminder that wealth is far from being merely what you can buy in the shops. Everybody is impoverished, to some extent, in a society that is collectively under-resourced; even the members of a wealthy elite, which can buy itself out of most difficulties, may feel the lack of social cohesiveness in a society in which some people are obliged to sleep in doorways; or they may sense their powerlessness in the face of environmental degradation or atmospheric pollution. Even in the world's richest societies there is plenty of work that needs doing, which society is unwilling either to organise or pay for.

Societies acknowledge that there are certain things best acquired collectively; roads, for example, and environmental protection measures, and maybe education and healthcare, too. In the UK (and typically in western societies) approaching half of the wealth that the country produces, as measured by GDP, is spent in this way. To pay for these, governments collect taxes, almost all of which are levied on transactions. The biggest ones arise when people are paid (income tax and National Insurance), and when they buy things (VAT and excise duty): the more transactions there are, the more money the government can get in. In an economy in which people built their own houses and grew their own vegetables, not much tax would be collected in this way.

Because it taxes transactions, the government has a strong interest in maintaining as much turnover in the economy as possible. Turnover, however, as we have seen, does not equate to true wealth-creation, and this focus on the circulation of wealth in the economy deprives a society of more effective opportunities for the creation of real wealth. The villain of the piece is Gross Domestic Product, or GDP, which was established as the internationally accepted measure of a country's economic performance following the Bretton Woods conference in 1944. GDP measures economic activity without regard to the welfare, wellbeing or capacity to flourish of a country's people arising from that activity. To emphasise the point, GDP ignores everything, including unpaid work, that is not part of a financial transaction, even though such work is almost invariably useful and wanted.

The value of a country's currency, which is closely linked to its ability to borrow money at competitive rates, is heavily influenced by whether its economy is growing or not, according to the GDP measure. In a democracy, a government's ability to spend money is critical to its electoral success, so its capacity to borrow at low rates and the amount of tax it can raise are its primary considerations. GDP growth is the key to both of these, with the promotion of the transactional economy strongly favoured because it has the "geometric" capacity for rapid growth. This is why the tax system targets transactions, rather than accumulated wealth: companies are the drivers of the transactional economy, so governments invariably favour shareholders and investors over people who work and spend.

In Britain, the evidence of how thoroughly the government has "bought in" to the transactional economy is nowhere stronger than in its unwavering support for the financial services industry, mostly centred upon the City of London. Here, there is no product as such; nothing is being created that is wanted or needed other than an opportunity to profit still further at the expense of others. The business of the financial services industry is pure transactional gain. Companies either make such gains for themselves or they charge fees to help others to do so; either way, the greater the number of transactional opportunities, the greater the gain. Trading shares, bonds, currencies, commodities and their derivatives, or simply lending money at a higher interest rate than is paid on it, or advising on the legal and accounting aspects of financial transactions and how best to avoid tax; these are all pseudo-products that do not add to the sum of human wellbeing. You cannot eat, drink, wear, seek shelter in or otherwise enjoy traded financial instruments. As real wealth-creation they are nothing: they merely rob Peter to pay Paul, and take a profit on the way.

Any rational society would want to keep this pseudo-productive activity to as little as possible, and yet financial services amount to 10% of the British economy, employing well over a million people,[1] figures that do not include the lawyers, accountants and other professional services upon which financial services depend. In the City of London, many of Britain's most able, determined and high-achieving people are tied up in the business of pushing wealth around the world, creaming off a proportion of it and concentrating it in the hands of a few, rather than making new, real wealth or helping others to do so. That such a resource of creative human potential is lost to the usefully productive economy is one sure reason why British manufacturing – once the world's pre-eminent – has declined drastically in size in the last forty years and lost its competitive and innovative edge.

Governments in Britain ritually celebrate the financial services sector as a great British success story, relying upon the contribution it make to the balance of the UK's exports. This balance is monstrously in deficit in relation to the trade in real things that people want and need, but for generations Britain has leveraged its historic commercial networks, paying for low priced physical goods with high cost transactional services in finance and business, thus continuing to hollow out its own productive core. This "export" in transactional costs, however, has no long-term benefits. Financial services depend upon people taking money from each other, rather than adding to the total sum of wealth, and for every gain a loss must eventually be borne by someone. For long periods rising asset values may mask the underlying losses and make everyone who owns assets feel richer. Eventually, however, the logic of trading in nothing proves unsustainable, and the location of losses abroad will not insulate Britain from the inevitable consequences of parading in the Emperor's new clothes. The cost to the British economy of the international banking collapse in 2008 remained, in 2014, a long way from being paid, but the financial services industry was unrepentant, asset values were

---

1   Maer L. and Broughton N., *Financial Services: contribution to the UK economy*, House of Commons Library, 21 August 2012

on the rise once more and GDP growth and the balance of payments were even more dependent upon transactional activity than before the crisis.

THE TRANSACTIONAL ECONOMY dictates the pattern of people's daily lives. They pay large amounts to travel to and from their place of work, and even larger sums to have their children looked after while they are there. OECD figures show that in 2012 two parents working full time in the UK would have spend nearly 30% of their net income on full-time care at a typical childcare centre for two children age 2 and 3, much higher than the EU average of 10%. These are transactional costs, where the transaction is represented by a person's employment. The wealth absorbed by making themselves available and then getting to their place of work requires people to seek to earn far more than they need simply to live.

In view of these costs, parents may choose to stay at home to look after their own children. This could take place in a social context, perhaps a community project where childcare is shared and unpaid but productive work such as growing food is undertaken. It is not so easy, however, to duck out of the transactional economy; dispensing with the paid childcare and commuting would be a big saving, but people are still faced with a large, non-discretionary item of household spending – the housing itself, the price of which is almost invariably dictated by the market. Houses are appreciating assets for their owners, whether owner-occupiers or landlords, and a transactional economy favours the accumulation of such assets over productive investment, such as plant and equipment, which depreciates. Depreciating assets are soon worth nothing, whereas assets that are capable of appreciation provide opportunities for repeated transactional returns.

Shares in companies, precious metals, works of art: the worth of all these is subject to the confidence that is generated by the willingness to buy and hold as an investment. Values become self-sustaining, underpinned by the conviction of desirability, which, when allied to the perception of rarity, creates the expectation of a capital return independently of any working income that may arise. In Britain, the value of land has become detached in this way from the working income that can reasonably be derived from it. Until 2008 the expectation was more or less hard-wired into social discourse that land in general and houses in particular would continue to increase in capital value, an expectation that rapidly reasserted itself in 2013. Ownership of a home has long been a key economic objective for many UK households. While the payment of rent is merely an expense, the payment of a mortgage appears as an investment, returning through the value of the property a large proportion of the money paid out.

The property market is the lock on Britain's transactional economy, since almost everyone who wants somewhere to live or work is obliged to participate. Rents, even social rents, reflect house prices to a great extent, while the high price of buildings and land has an impact across the economy, upon any activity that needs to take place on land and / or under a roof. The price of food reflects the cost of farmland; the prices in shops and restaurants reflect the high rents that retail premises command; hotel prices, which in Britain have long been notably high, reflect directly the cost of the land on which the hotel stands. And so it goes on: land is the ultimate repository of surplus wealth in the economy, its cost set not by objective value but by the maximum that its users are able to afford.

In a market economy, "objective value" and "the maximum that its users are able to afford" may appear to be the same thing. It is only with reference to what people are prepared to pay that a market price can be established. But the market also distorts decision-making and outcomes; house-buyers typically stretch their budget to the maximum, and then try to make their other domestic and personal expenditure fit around what remains. Similarly, a shopkeeper is forced to pay the maximum rent that any sort of retail activity could achieve on their premises. The social utility of the activity is neither here nor there in this calculation; wholly transactional activities such as banks, estate agents and bookmakers set the market, while bookshops and specialist food outlets (among others) struggle with the resulting level of rent.

Ownership of land is connected to the human need for permanence and belonging, not to mention the feelings of self-esteem and status that inspired 18th century landowners in their grand projects. Home improvement is a major pre-occupation of house-owners; it drives a big industry for DIY products, underpinned by an often mistaken belief that the money people spend is contributing to the value of their asset. The disjunct between property prices and retail prices is stark in this respect: rising house prices are considered a positive thing, reported in the media as evidence of optimism that the economy is doing well. Rising retail prices, however, are characterised negatively as inflationary, or evidence that the economy is not producing as efficiently as it should. The picture that fuels this – that money laid out on owned property is not spent, as such, but safely stored for the future – takes no account of how the cost of land sucks wealth out of the economy, locking it up where it cannot be used and requiring people to work much harder than they otherwise would in order to replace it.

All this is good news for GDP. The incentive (or obligation) for people to do more paid work to meet their financial commitments, the money people spend on their houses and the opportunities for increased borrowing that ride on the back of high property prices all keep money turning over in the economy to register GDP growth. Travelling to work, and employing childcare in order to be able to do so, creates GDP in the work of the child minder and the train drivers, car mechanics and petrol retailers who keep people on the move. Both the wages paid and the expenditure on travel attract taxes, too, so the government is happy. Neither the unpaid childcare of a stay-at-home parent, however, nor any increase in the wellbeing of child and parent from their time together, nor the value of any unpaid work they may do in the community, has a GDP or tax value. GDP is a function of the price of activity, not its usefulness, and its growth depends upon people leading excessively busy, transactional lives. The desire to achieve more in life by doing less in financial terms runs contrary to the prevailing political and economic framework.

Here is the reason why Keynes' prediction to his grandchildren has proved so wrong. The prescription for growth and prosperity that the western world applied to itself at Bretton Woods in 1944 depended not upon the creation of real wealth, but the turnover of money. Governments were committed to making people work as much as possible to maximise turnover, not as little as possible to supply their human needs. Transactional activity is the only type of work capable of growing at the exponential rate necessary to keep up in the international race on which Bretton Woods fired the starting pistol, because there is no logical limit to the amount of such work that people can be expected to do. The way that the economy creams off surplus wealth in the form of profit, then locks it up in increasing asset values, is an essential part of the deal since it guards against economic satiety or complacency – the risk that people in significant numbers feel sufficiently wealthy that they opt out of money-making work.

The pay-off for this settlement is the instant gratification of conspicuous consumption. The extent of shops and restaurants, measured by square metres of retail space per person, increased by a third between 1974 and 2008, without taking into account the online presence that now accounts for 20% or more of shopping. In 2012, over 10% of the working population was employed in the retail trade. For the many people who appreciate spending their money in enticing sales environments, stocked with a large range and serviced by plenty of staff, this is an attractive outcome. Like eating out, shopping is a leisure activity in its own right – something that people want to do almost independently of the pleasure and usefulness to be gained from the products they buy.

This activity, however, comes at a cost, which is far greater that the people enjoying it are likely to be aware. Retailing is one of the largest transactional sectors of the British economy – second only to financial and business services in the transactional gain that arises from it. A good 40% of spending on shopping and eating out pays for the activity, rather than the things bought or consumed. The entire industry runs on low pay: taken collectively, British retailing has eviscerated British manufacturing by sourcing its goods ever more cheaply from abroad, and has replaced many of those manufacturing jobs with cheap retail labour, much of which is non-specialised and therefore unskilled.

The result for the retail companies is lower input prices, higher margins and increased sales; a no-less important consequence for society is that people have lost touch with the true value of goods because they no longer make them, or no longer know people who work in manufacturing trades. Just as children are sometimes reported not to understand that milk comes from cows, or that crisps are made from potatoes that once grew in the earth, so contemporary shoppers have little connection with the origin of the goods that they buy. In assessing quality and desirability, Britain's shoppers are held hostage by the label, brand and sticker price.

A transactional society is skilled at comparing labels, but the challenges it faces in evaluating true worth have implications way beyond the supermarket aisle. How may it estimate, for example, the relative merits of collectively employing half a million extra shop assistants, compared with a similar number of additional teachers to enhance children's education or nurses and care home assistants to improve the life conditions of the elderly? The latter appear like a cost to be paid for collectively from the public purse through the taxes levied on transactions, whereas the former appears to be a free benefit that the transactional economy obligingly supplies. In the economy of real goods and services, however, containing the things that people want and need, the opposite is the case. Education and care of the elderly are real goods, while extra shop assistants increase the cost of purchases.

The decision is not a straightforward one in the terms stated, but is a question of social direction that government, a key conspirator in the transactional economy, must find a way to address. In Britain, politics since the 1970s has focused strongly on the individual consumption and social wealth; the Bretton Woods prescriptions for rebuilding the global economy after the Second World War are no longer relevant, because the questions are different. Yet the competitive economic incentives to keep wealth circulating profitably through the economy remain in place and have been strongly augmented.

The already wealthy are encouraged to enrich themselves still further in the hope that some of that additional wealth will "trickle down" through the money-go-round. Economic theorists have convinced politicians that success in this way is just a matter of the correct manipulation of the levers. To that end there have been tax rises, tax cuts, tax credits, tax incentives, minimum wages, fiscal stimulus, devaluation, interest rate management, quantitative easing, regulation, de-regulation, nationalisation, privatisation, competition, mutualisation, de-mutualisation, education reform, healthcare reform, local government reform, indeed reform of pretty much everything that the government touches in order to discover the ideal combination of parameters that will optimise the workings of the social "machine". Through all of this the primary policy driver has been GDP growth, which means that the focus has been upon increasing money-based activity of any sort rather than productive activity that is useful in the human sense.

Those levers are the problem, since they allow politicians to believe that there is a technocratic, management solution to a question that is essentially human in scope. The transactional economy, so enormously wasteful of human effort, comes about as a result of a social and political convention that dictates that people should seek to make their wealth *out of* each other, rather than *with* each other. How to change this is the challenge for politics in the 21st century. The question itself is simple: as less and less human work is required in production, how will the real wealth of wellbeing be shared out in a way that meets everybody's needs?

For a society to perfect the distribution of wealth, innate human qualities of collaboration will be needed across every aspect of people's lives. This means not a new round of socialist proscription but a new approach to accessing the power for good that lies within the human will. The relationships that link people's economic activity are no different to their interpersonal relationships more generally. If society can support people in their innate capacity to manage these relationships, there is at least some hope that a human solution to the problem of wealth sharing can emerge.

Chapter 6

MADE FOR SHARING?

The politics of wealth, and its beneficiaries

LONG BEFORE BILL Clinton won the 1992 U.S. presidential election on the basis that "It's the economy, stupid", politicians in democratic countries had discovered that a growing economy is the key to electoral success. Growth creates jobs, which give people access to a share in national wealth. People with a sufficient share in national wealth are happy because they can buy the goods and services that they need. They also pay taxes, which allows the government to provide the public services that people want. It is a virtuous circle, in which more growth equals more jobs equals more wealth shared around.

The key phrase in this paragraph is "a sufficient share in national wealth". In a developed economy such as Britain's, relatively few jobs create real wealth. More and more just push it round the system, so that, on average, there is less wealth for each of them to cream off in this way. The distribution is also very uneven: a complicated tax system, for example, does not create new wealth, but it certainly creates well-paid jobs for tax collectors, tax lawyers and accountants, adequately paid jobs for their secretaries and the people who programme their computers, and poorly paid jobs for the people who clean their offices and make and deliver the sandwiches they eat at their desks. Accountancy and law are booming areas of business: membership of accountancy bodies increased by 56% in the 15 years to 2012,[1] while the Law Society reported in 2011[2] that in the previous 30 years – a

---

1   Data derived from *Key Facts and Trends in the Accountancy Profession*, Financial Reporting Council, various years
2   *Trends in the solicitors' profession*, Annual statistical report 2011

period during which the population rose by 13% – the total number of solicitors in England and Wales holding practising certificates
grew by 206%. The hierarchy of jobs they have created give people
access to a share in national wealth depending on their status. But
the productive wealth is created by other people, many of whom are
poorly paid.

Tax collection and avoidance are transactional activities in an
increasingly transactional economy; indeed the growth in the number of solicitors, accountants, bankers, investment managers, con-
sultants, estate agents, financial advisers and regulatory government
agencies is symptomatic of an economy in which there are more –
and more complicated – transactions than ever before. Whereas one
solicitor was sufficient for 1200 people in 1981, by 2011 nearly three
were needed, suggesting not that life had got better, but more complicated, and people were having to buy a lot more legal services
than they did. Even GDP growth could not explain this increase; GDP
more or less doubled over the period, so the tripling in the number of
solicitors suggests that the economy had become more transactional
in that time.

Transactions underpin the competitive nature of a market economy, in which each person tries to emerge with the greatest advantage. People employ advisers to negotiate on their behalf, either to
maximise their gain or to convince themselves that they have done
so. Competitiveness of this sort is assumed to be innate to economic
activity in a free society. It keeps everybody on their toes and ensures
that the economy operates as efficiently as possible. But competition engages people in different ways. Some compete to get ahead,
and are willing to take risks as they do so. Many, however, are far
more concerned about falling behind, so they are put off collaborating freely by the fear of others "taking advantage" by not pulling
their weight in a collaborative task.

People may experience this in personal terms as a loss to themselves, but to characterise such a breakdown in relationship as competitive is a misuse of the term. The desire not to be taken advantage
of comes from a collaborative place that has equality as its touch-

stone, which explains why the trades union movement grew to such strength in Europe during the post-war years. At its centre was a picture of economic competition not between individual working people (the survival of the fittest) but between working people as a group, on the one hand, and, on the other, the much smaller, risk-taking group who sought to acquire as much wealth as possible from the work that other people do.

According to this view, competitiveness is not innate to economic activity and relationships in a free society, but has been built into it by the dominance of a minority of the competitively-inclined. These risk-takers, in aspiring to the social and political status associated with economic gain, compete among each other for the best opportunities to make profits, the chief source of which are the less competitively-inclined majority. Individual gain has long been the driving force of social mobility, and there is nothing fixed about the composition of the aspirant group. But even while some prosper, many others are dragged unwillingly into a competition for which they lack the necessary temperament and resources.

This is not the way that the politically-engaged and inter-connected worlds of high-level business, the media, and even politics itself, sees things. These worlds contain a relatively higher proportion of risk-takers, with the power to project a self-serving image of society that celebrates entrepreneurship and the profit motive as the creators of national prosperity. So successful has this been, that they are now in a position to demand that economic policy is focused upon incentivising them to do even better. There is some evidence that this group is characterised by distinctive behavioural and character traits; a 2010 study by Dr Robert Hare suggests that 4% of senior business managers display psychopathic tendencies, compared with 1% of the population as a whole. Psychopathic or not, the behaviour of the ascendant minority tends towards a competitive social and economic framework in which the majority are cast in an economically passive and vulnerable role.

There is nothing new about this. When William of Normandy raised an army, sailed to England and destroyed the English King

Harold's forces at the Battle of Hastings, he did so entrepreneurially. The death of Edward the Confessor had created uncertainty over the succession from which William believed that he could profit by taking a risk. That risk was high: Harold was not the loser that popular history has portrayed him; he very nearly prevailed at Hastings, even though he had just seen off a rival Norwegian invasion in a battle two hundred miles to the north. The gain, however, for William, and the knights who speculated their own lives and that of their retinues by joining his expedition, was enormous. The new king had the whole of the lands of England with which to pay a dividend to his investors.

Warfare was to the mediaeval nobility much as business is to contemporary elites; it provided opportunities for the strongest and most determined to advance in wealth and power, and called upon the same risk-embracing personality traits. Military conflict, as a means to promote lordly honour, personal gain and religious orthodoxy, dominated the history of mediaeval and early modern Europe, but the interplay between warfare, political power, religion and the accumulation of wealth has by no means disappeared in the contemporary world. The "war on terror" unleashed after 2001 has made and broken political careers, increased the power of governments to enquire into and direct the lives of their citizens, provided profitable contracts for companies in the "security" and armaments sectors (among many others) and conveyed more than a hint of moral ascendancy over an enemy identified largely on the basis of religion. The geo-political objectives of this war may not have been achieved, but the sense of jeopardy it has engendered has helped to instil a culture of social and political dependency. Since the threat of nuclear holocaust that hovered over the Cold War has declined, the war on terror has provided a new channel in which political and economic elites may combine to impose their authority upon the less assertive.

Attempts to address the social harms that flow from this dependency reach far back into history, popularised in the tales of Robin Hood and much more grimly realised through systems of public relief such as those established by the English Poor Laws between the 16th and the 19th centuries. The problems of rural poverty, however, although extensive, were rapidly eclipsed by conditions in Britain's growing industrial cities, where a much more visible and explicit picture of deprivation and exploitation could be discerned, something that could no longer be managed on a local or piecemeal scale. The origins of socialism as a political movement are to be found in these conditions, the cause of the problem clearly identified in the mismatch in power between the owners of the capital required to purchase the means of production and the workers who carried out the production itself. The bond of mutual dependency between landowner and worker that had provided some cohesiveness to the rural economy was far less strong in an industrial society where both capital and labour were fluid. Since the former was free to seek out the best returns wherever they arose, the latter was inevitably vulnerable to insecurity and greater exploitation.

The trades union movement emerged alongside socialism as a counterweight to the power of capital; its approach, seeking better pay and conditions for workers through co-ordinated negotiations backed by the threat of the withdrawal of labour, was directed at rebalancing the relationship between labour and capital rather than building an effective collaboration between the two. A more idealistic vision of socialism appeared to be advanced when, between the Second World War and the 1970s, many major industries in Britain were taken into public ownership. Rather than placing industrial workers in control of their own productive activity, however, the government and its industrial agencies became mired in the role of capital-owning employer, creating an ideological minefield that culminated in the confrontations of the 1970s and early '80s. Meanwhile, the totalitarian model of socialism practised in the Soviet Union, China and their satellites succeeded in stripping out the competitive incentives of a free market economy without replacing them with anything more truly reflective of human motivations.

The totalitarian socialist experiment ground to a halt with the fall of the Berlin Wall, the raising of the Iron Curtain and the adoption in China of the main principles of market capitalism – developments

greeted by some in the west as harbingers of "the end of history"[1]
– code for the final discrediting of Marxist dialectics in favour of
the unchanging certainties of liberal democracy, capitalism and the
market system. The totalitarian regimes had implemented socialist
ideals so poorly that any potential there might have been for willing
human co-operation on the heroic scale envisaged had little chance
of finding real expression. Taken as a whole, socialism failed because,
in attempting to manage economic activity in the interests of society,
it had no mechanism beyond ideology or *diktat* to decide what those
interests were. In all its manifestations, therefore, it tended towards
a one-size-fits-all approach that could not address effectively the specific and varied needs and wants of individual people.

In contrast, the "selfish" model of capitalism practised in the west
fared rather better, both morally and in practice, on the strength of its
underpinning with the rhetoric of freedom. For as long as restrictions
on social, political and economic freedoms prevailed in the Soviet
and Chinese dictatorships, this rhetoric had considerable traction.
The resulting conflation of freedom with market capitalism gave rise,
however, to a victor's interpretation of history as the "triumph of capitalism", which gave renewed respectability to unbridled individual
gain. Here was a missed opportunity, since both models had failed to
some extent. The capitalist west was far richer that the Communist
bloc, but many people within the west's sphere of influence had been
left behind in its march of progress. The preferred outcome of the collapse of Communism would have been one in which both sides were
willing to learn. As it was, everybody who could, from the well placed
Soviet apparatchiks turned kleptocrats to the profit-hungry western
corporations in search of cheap labour, know-how and raw materials,
were too busy pillaging the under-utilised resources of Eastern Europe
and the former USSR to pay any attention. Where Communism had
attempted to focus, with limited success, on the production of real
wealth, the "triumphant" west found itself ideologically committed
to a system that prioritised the freedom to pursue profit over truly

1   See Fukuyama F.,*The End of History and the Last Man,*1992

productive work. It had fallen victim to its own Cold War rhetoric and was blinded to the weaknesses of the approach it was taking.

For a while these weaknesses were well concealed. A consumption-driven economic boom was fuelled by the cheap labour available to producers in the Far East; China, in particular, ran up huge trade balances that it was only too happy to lend back to the west to keep the orders flowing. While credit was plentiful, the fact that so much of western economic activity was essentially unproductive could conveniently be ignored. Banks were able to inflate their profits through rising asset values, including the notorious "securitised mortgages", many of which were taken out by people who had little hope of sustaining the repayments. While house prices were rising the ability to repay was not an issue: a borrower in default could always sell up, pay off the mortgage and probably still walk away with a profit. So long as the money flowed people lived for the present and failed to contemplate the impending risks.

Only when house prices stopped rising, as they did in 2008, and then began to fall, did the bubble burst with spectacular effect. Those unsustainable mortgages collapsed in value, leaving the banks nursing enormous losses. A chain reaction set in, threatening to destroy the capital base of many of the west's largest financial institutions; governments felt obliged first to rescue the banks and then to seek to kick-start stalled economies with large injections of additional cash. This was market failure on a grand scale, from which those with stored wealth were rescued at the expense of taxpayers following unprecedented government intervention. Coming, as it did, in the wake of the pivotal events of 9/11 and the global "war on terror" that it precipitated, the financial shock of 2008 effectively destroyed the myth that the market had taken over from history as the determining force in human development. The capacity of history to pull surprises had been powerfully reasserted, along with the centrality of government intervention to people's lives.

THE IDEALS OF socialism had the briefest of flowerings in western politics. The short interval between 1945 and the mid-1970s – the span of a single generation – is the only sustained period in British history when the distribution of wealth between the better and the less well-off was altered appreciably in the latter's favour by political means. Since the 1980s the tendency has been inexorably in the other direction, for although the fall from grace of ideological socialism has only slightly reduced the redistributive principle in government policy, that "slightly" has made a big difference at the extremes. The pressure, in a profits-driven economy, for the rich to get richer while the poor get poorer is so intense that it takes a concerted and sustained effort to reverse it. In the absence of that effort the redistributive activity has continued to much lesser effect.

In Britain, as in all developed economies, the majority of the money the government raises through taxation is spent either on cash payments to the needy or on providing services that the less well off could not otherwise afford. Foremost of these are health and education, essentially personal services that wealthier people may choose to buy from private providers, reinforcing a perception that the government provision is under-resourced or of lower quality. Nonetheless, in 2012 health and education accounted for £221 billion of government spending – over a third of the total excluding debt interest. Cash benefits, including the state pension, were a further £207 billion, while other services and subsidies added another £55 billion or so. In round terms, a good three quarters of government spending, which itself accounts for roughly 45% of GDP, has a broadly redistributive intention, where "redistributive" means that if people already owned a sufficient share of the national wealth such government spending would not be necessary. By contrast, traditional government spending on defence and public order amounted to £71 billion, or about 11% of the total.

Some of this spending provides a form of insurance, which seeks to share out an unequal risk. The National Health Service, for example, when well run, has proved an efficient method of distributing universal healthcare, but even so people who can afford it prefer to buy health insurance from private firms. Most government spending, however, has straightforward value: for a family with three children, the state pays about £30,000[1] per year for their education, which for many families is significantly more than they earn. Although some pension and child benefits go to people who could easily do without them, the majority represents a simple cash transfer from the better- to the less-well-off. Like it or not, most government spending is in principle profoundly redistributive – to make provision for people who otherwise would not be able to manage for themselves.

Most of this redistribution is politically uncontroversial. The coalition government that came to power in 2010 may have sought to save odd bits of money by vilifying "welfare scroungers" and forcing the unemployed into unrewarding work, but it has talked-up spending on both health and education and would not dream of alienating the vote-rich pensioner lobby. The principle of collectivism, therefore, that emerged from 19th and 20th century social reforms, remains firmly embedded in the modern British state. The idea that national wealth is something in which all are entitled to participate is a staple of political rhetoric from both left and right. The reason is obvious: in a democracy underpinned by universal suffrage, there are far more winners than losers from a redistributive approach.

The key phrase identified at the beginning of the chapter – "a sufficient share in national wealth" to which people aspire – is indeed, therefore, the primary objective of western democratic politics. The debate about how to achieve this has, however, narrowed greatly since the free market became established as the only economic model, and GDP as the only way of measuring it. This "GDP first" approach makes a crude assumption that more money wealth created in an economy means more real wealth to go round. We have seen that this is flawed, for two reasons. First, so much of the wealth measured by GDP is transactional gain, not real, productive wealth, and much wealth that is real is not measured by GDP; second, when more wealth flows into an economy it does not readily "go round",

1   An approximation based upon a budget of £90bn and c. 9m school-age children

but tends to accumulate in a limited number of bank accounts or use-lessly disappear into inflated asset values. Nonetheless, maximising GDP has become a pre-condition to any political conversation about how the national wealth should be spent, which helps to explain why the economic policies of Thatcher, Blair and the Conservative / Liberal Democrat coalition have varied so little.

The right has the better of the "GDP-first" approach, since overall growth on the GDP measure is most easily achieved in a transactional economy that maximises individual personal gain. The more egalitarian left has been forced into various contortions such as the "Third Way", championed by the Blair government to match unfettered market capitalism with a social agenda. This New Labour attempt to combine a right wing approach to wealth creation with a socially inspired approach to spending had unfortunate consequences. While a left wing government was cheered on by the right in the rush to transactional growth, no one within the political spectrum had eyes open for the trouble ahead.

By far the worst recent excesses of capitalism in the UK were initiated in the Blair years, when private enterprise was encouraged to take risks and enter corners of the economy and public life of which the Thatcher government could only dream. The problem, however, was that the measures taken to encourage individual wealth, such as low capital and business taxes, meant that sufficient additional wealth to spend on social projects was not available when times got hard. The high command of New Labour was notoriously "relaxed about people getting filthy rich", and great emphasis was placed upon the trickle-down effect, which asserted that as society got richer overall, everyone would benefit. For a brief moment it appeared to be so: the New Labour period saw a significant reduction in child poverty indicators, for example, in the days of plenty when crumbs really did fall from rich men's tables. But those days were all too few, and the subsequent events catastrophic. Since so much of the wealth was neither real nor useful, it disappeared in a puff of smoke when the credit bubble burst.

The Third Way epitomised the narrowness of the economic debate permitted under "GDP first" rules, a narrowness that persisted as Britain attempted to extract itself from a sequence of recessions. Nonetheless, vestiges remain of the traditional left-right duality: the right-wing coalition that came to power in 2010 were determined that reducing government spending would ensure the long-term stability of the economy and secure inward private investment. Coupled to this were lower taxes on profit-making activities, and opportunities to employ workers more cheaply, both intended to bring an increase in economic activity despite their dampening effect on government finances, reducing tax income and placing a greater burden on the welfare state. In contrast, the left considered that increased government spending was required to stimulate economic activity, and that the time to pay off the debts would be when this had been achieved.

Reducing government spending is code for withdrawing the state from control of the economy and letting the market get on with it. Increasing government spending to stimulate economic activity smacks of greater interference and the expectation that, somehow or another, the successful will have to pay. The dilemma highlighted by the Third Way was the incompatibility of the two interest groups that these approaches seek to serve. A destructive tension underlay the New Labour attempt to reconcile the ambitious, risk-taking minority with the risk-averse majority. By courting the former, they lost touch with the true interests of the latter; as so often in politics, far too little account was taken of how people actually are, with decisions taken and policies rashly introduced based on how politicians and economists would like people to be. The pain was augmented when politicians then tried to mould human behaviour to meet their expectations. In its attempts to manage this, Blair's was probably the most controlling peacetime government modern Britain has experienced. By one count it introduced 3,000 new criminal offences in as many days, while leveraging the "war on terror" to make significant inroads into long-established freedoms of the individual in relation to the power of the state.

MANAGING THE RELATIONSHIP between politics and human behaviour is a key aspect of human politics. The choices and decisions that people make are filtered through a range of complex human motivations, which rarely accord with the unerring self-interest of classical economic theory. Experimental studies repeatedly prove what people know from their own experience, that they routinely place their economic interests second to the wellbeing they derive from kind, selfless and generous acts. They are also shown to be bad decisionmakers when working out where their economic self-interest really lies. Either way, they are vulnerable to people and organisations such as commercial companies whose economic self-interest is more coldly calculated. A society that encourages people to get as rich as they can in the mistaken belief that everyone will prosper is increasing that vulnerability, while taking upon itself the cost and responsibility of correcting its subsequent ills. Such a society is deliberately making problems that it then has to fix.

How can society make space for everybody to live in prosperity, without the problems that arise when people attempt to exploit one another for personal gain? The answer lies not in trying to force, mould or even persuade everybody into a common economic model, such as market capitalism, or command socialism, or even the more agreeable-sounding co-operativism, but to accommodate different, co-existent models in ways that reflect different human temperaments and motivations and do not seek to outdo one another. Society need neither, for example, encourage nor condemn someone who wishes to become as rich as they can; it may simply accept it, provided that person does not operate through the exploitation of others. Such exploitation creates a problem that society then needs to solve, so it is entitled to prevent it happening; it is equally entitled to smooth the paths of people who wish to create useful wealth on equal terms, since this solves rather than creates social problems.

Because there is only so much that a government can do, this approach to problem-solving depends not upon creating a certain sort of social framework, but upon framing policy in a way that minimises the subsequent interventions that government has to make. For example, the traditional right wing aspiration to "small government", or "government that does not interfere in people's lives" is poorly served by the alternative that it points to, of having the market sort out people's economic relationships. Because people are so different, the market creates enormous distributive inequalities that the government then has to correct through comprehensive intervention. In general, a much smaller early intervention may prevent a problem occurring that, once it has taken hold, can only be solved with a large intervention. Prevention is better than cure, and small government is more likely to be achieved by setting, at the outset, more proscriptive ground-rules to prevent market inequality from getting out of control.

With this in mind, government policy should favour human organisations that reduce the problems that it has to solve. It could, for example, levy lower taxes on "good" companies that pay their employees (and those in their supply chains) well enough for them not to require state benefits to supplement their income; or that facilitate time off for them to look after their children, elderly relations, and so forth. Care of the elderly and the consequences of inadequate child-rearing are, after all, both problems that the state must try to solve if people are not able to do so for themselves. Any wealth-creating organisation has a number of ways of measuring its output, of which shareholder dividend is probably the least useful in solving the challenges that society faces. The health and wellbeing of its employees and their families is another such measure, and a company that can sustain this consistently is no less successful (and much more socially useful) than one whose dividends increase year on year.

Tax policy is a blunt instrument that can achieve certain things, but a more fundamental re-think is needed in order to minimise the amount of wealth-redistribution and social problem-solving that government must undertake. At present, for example, all companies benefit from limited liability – a market intervention by government that encourages corporate risk-takers by limiting their potential losses and allowing them to escape liability for any subsequent debts. Reserving this status for companies that measure their success and output in terms of social good rather than shareholder dividend would cause other, profit-focused companies to be much more wary of the risks they had previously expected society to share. Changing the rules in this way would also channel entrepreneurship into socially useful directions. It might well reduce the total amount of measurable activity in the economy on the GDP measure, but it would increase the proportion of socially useful, truly productive activity while decreasing transactional activity that exists only to cream off an investor return.

Underlying this proposal is a yet more fundamental need to redefine the terms in which economic activity is measured. People naturally want to succeed, but whereas an individual's ambitions and intentions change continually with their circumstances, human organisations need to to spell out appropriate success criteria around which people can combine their talents, urge each other on and be held to account. These terms of success require regular review: at present governments globally are gauging their economic performance against a measure designed to optimise output in the U.S. economy during the Second World War, some 70 or more years ago. Among many, many bizarre consequences, a nurse employed to look after an elderly person, or a child minder to look after a toddler, both increase the success of society on the standard measure of GDP, whereas an extended family or community group, in which such activities are shared out without exchange of money, counts for nothing. A gun is equivalent to a ploughshare in GDP measurement, even though one is for growing food and the other is for killing people.

GDP had some relevance to an economy engaged in total war. Human wellbeing, social benefit and the depletion of natural resources, none of which GDP measures, could legitimately be considered secondary when government policy was focused on getting as many people as possible to be active in the national task. The existence of such a task greatly assisted government in organisational terms; it allowed it to intervene and prioritise in ways that governments have continued to adopt in peacetime. During the Cold War, the U.S. and its economic allies sought to demonstrate the superiority of the western market economy over the Communist system by maximising economic output and winning the technological arms race; since then, the focus has been upon keeping up with or outdoing "global competitors", applying language that characterises life on this planet as a constant battle for economic supremacy among nation states.

The agreed success criteria that drive human organisations need to be reviewed regularly not just for their methodologies but also for their objectives. The former is an economist's and the latter a politician's task. The economists have kept to their part enthusiastically, making regular modifications to the GDP yardstick in order to measure money transactions with greater finesse. Political establishments have, however, rarely permitted themselves to question the yardstick's underlying relevance to contemporary societies. So far from reassessing the 70 year old objectives of GDP measurement, they have merely encouraged the economists to reinforce them. This has included finding new evidence of wealth-production in some of the arcane areas of transactional activity that led almost directly to the financial melt-down of 2008.[1]

Applied to a technologically mature economy in the 21st century, where the capacity to produce sufficient wealth is not in issue, the way in which GDP is measured distorts policy in directions that require massive subsequent intervention by government to correct them. In particular, it frames policy to get as many people as possible into as much paid work as possible, irrespective of whether that work is truly productive or even necessary and conducive to the individual and collective good. Throughout government, the baleful influence of the political imperative to maximise GDP can be felt. Perhaps the most extreme example is found in education policy, where the development of social and cultural capital have been gradually marginalised by government reforms that took hold in the 1980s. These place a strong emphasis on basic functional skills to the detriment of deeper personal development, and are rigorously enforced through a reductive system of school and pupil assessment aimed at producing

---

1   See Fioramonti, L., *Gross Domestic Problem*, London, 2013, page 111

a supply of readily employable people to join the GDP treadmill.

GDP is not an absolute or accurate or even useful measure of a society's wealth production; it is merely the measure that governments and their executive officers have been given, to which they hold with extreme tenacity because they are "success" driven. Established success criteria for human organisations, although necessary, often have a dangerous hold over their participants, who may readily subordinate their individual better judgement out of loyalty, dependency or susceptibility to an uncritical group-think. This is why policy makers have failed the challenge set by Keynes in his letter to his grandchildren, of a 15 hour working week by the early 21st century It is not because there is not enough wealth in total for this to happen, but because most people are not able to get access to a sufficient share. Because the success criteria of GDP are stuck in a very different past, the only solution available to the government is a "war economy", forcing people to work more and more in an effort to create yet more transactional gain.

IT SEEMS SELF-EVIDENT that the economic success criteria that a government would wish to apply are those that reflect the best outcomes for the wellbeing of society's members. They would seek to reflect how people really are, and the way they choose to live, rather than a government or society-approved notion of how they should be. It *would* seem self-evident, were this not belied by the absolute novelty of the proposal. There is scarcely any precedent in history for a government ruling on this basis, chiefly because no society until recently has had the potential to be so economically free. Now, however, the effort required for a technologically mature and well organised society to provide for its basic needs – the needs that in earlier times it took people a whole life's effort to sustain – is a small part of its total capacity to enhance its wellbeing. The problems to which market capitalism and Communism brought such different answers – the problems of increasing a society's wealth-producing capacity – have succumbed, in technical terms, to mechanisation and automation. The problem we are left with is the political expression of this technical achievement: how all the individuals in society, rather than merely a small elite, may use their time and energy creatively and with fulfilment, to live flourishing lives.

The future of a technologically proficient society can only be, as Keynes foresaw, that people need labour less to produce the essentials for existence. In trying to maximise the amount of paid work that everyone does, therefore, government *policy* is addressing the problem of a former age. Government *activity*, however, which is best characterised by the things that it spends its money on, is another matter. The British government is currently appropriating and spending at least a third of national wealth in attempting to correct the difficulties that the economic system – the system that it supports as a matter of policy – is creating. That figure may be close to the limit of intervention achievable in a free democracy, and is still palpably failing to meet the scale of social and economic difficulty with which government is faced. Logic suggests that it is not the lack of effort that is the problem, or even the lack of money, but that government is doing *the wrong thing*, intervening in the wrong way on account of the inappropriate success criteria to which it clings.

A truly successful government would do not as much as possible, but as little as necessary, commensurate with enabling people to flourish together in their own different ways. It would organise things so that positive human qualities, expressed in the innate human capacity for social self-organisation, were first of all empowered to operate to their fullest possible extent with a minimum of subsequent intervention from the state. To do this, government really does need to start from a true understanding of how people are, and this is the subject of the next chapter.

Chapter 7

THE LIMITS OF DEMOCRACY

Recovering personal autonomy in a regulatory age

COLONEL FITZWILLIAM (RETIRED) drives into his local town every day to buy a newspaper. He parks on the High Street and pops into the newsagent for a few minutes. Sometimes he visits the bank or the post office, too.

The signs on the roadside say *1 hour parking; no return within two hours*. Or they used to say that; now they read *1 hour maximum; pay at meter*, with a little arrow pointing in the direction of the nearest one. Shopkeepers complained that cars sometimes stayed for more than an hour, which was considered bad for trade; so the Council decided to install payment meters with tickets to show the time that people arrive. This made the system easier to enforce, while also raising money to pay for the people who do the enforcing.

Surveys showed that there was very little change in people's behaviour as a result of the meters, and this was mostly because people like the colonel, who park for only a few minutes, did not bother with the new system. He did not think it worth walking 20 yards down the street to buy a ticket, even supposing that he had the correct change, when it would merely mean that he was taking up a parking space for longer. The way he saw it, charges were introduced to deter people from overstaying the one hour limit, which he never did. In truth, the very normality of the situation, pulling up by the pavement, nipping into a shop and nipping out again, was such that he – and many like him – gave the matter little thought. Until, that is, one day the colonel got caught in a queue at the bank and returned to find a penalty notice taped to his windscreen. Was he entitled to be furious? In one sense he was "bang to rights", but even so the punishment did not advance the cause that it intended. It did not stop him from abusing the one hour limit, since he never did so; but it did provoke him to buy his paper at a petrol station on the by-pass, and to go into town less often. Since the petrol station is owned by a multi-national oil company this is one more loss to the local economy that the new parking arrangements were supposed to defend.

THE COLONEL'S STORY, trivial in itself, is familiar to millions who have innocently transgressed an arbitrary rule. Multiplied by those millions it well characterises the political process that has played out in Britain in the post-war era, for it highlights a distinction between the expectations that contemporary democratic processes encourage and the way in which people naturally behave.

The original parking arrangements were flexible and forgiving, which is how many people try to be in their personal lives. They encouraged sharing, and were generally tolerant of human circum-stances. People might, like the colonel, have been stuck in a queue; or they may have been struggling with bags of shopping and a recal-citrant toddler; or they may have been subject to any of a thousand other human eventualities, none of them associated with a desire to "take advantage" of other people wishing to park in the town. In the public, democratic space, however, consideration of the human circumstances and motivations that form people's actions is discour-aged in favour of a strict and impartial application of rules. That is how the Council likes it; the complaints they received about parking have metamorphosed into a new revenue stream from ticket sales and fines. The government is happy, too, because something that once was free is now paid for, which gives a boost to GDP. This tech-nocratic solution, however, to a problem that was essentially human in nature, comes at a cost in human integrity. The creation of new rules mean that more people are likely to break them, whether they intend to or not, while the capacity to adjust behaviour in response to circumstances and the needs of others is discounted as of little value.

The forms of modern democracy encourage people to occupy the public space. Politicians and officials are influenced by the representations they receive, which gives a disproportionally strong voice to the determined and articulate. Just as three tailors in Tooley Street, in London, once famously petitioned the British government with the phrase "We, the people of England...", so may any public representation carry an association with the popular will. A small number of complaints may easily be talked up into a generalised public concern. This multiplying effect, in which small specific experiences rapidly transform into a widespread general experience, is found everywhere in modern political discourse, providing justification for policy solutions of dubious intellectual or practical worth.

The victim of all of this is human autonomy – the opportunity for people to make decisions for themselves about how they relate to their fellows. The people of Colonel Fitzwilliam's town proved publicly unwilling to embrace human fallibility in the way that they would in their personal relationships. They dis-empowered themselves by a process of a hundred casual conversations and secondhand critiques, permitting an inflexible parking control system to be imposed that would henceforth be a cost to themselves. When the autonomy of human relationships is surrendered, there is always somebody willing to come up with an arbitrary framework of regulations to take their place. From their place in the public realm, people are strangely willing to allow this to happen. By the time they realise the consequences for their personal experience, it is usually too late to do anything about it.

Immigration and asylum policies provide repeated examples of this at a national level. Here is one of those generalised issues, providing a ready opportunity for people occupying the public realm to blame outsiders for a community's woes. Individual people, however, really don't like it when their actual immigrant neighbours, who may have been years in the community, are suddenly removed by force channelled through some faceless state agency. People may be against immigration in general, but they want to keep the immigrants whom they know and talk to, and with whose children their own children play. The differences that divide rapidly give way to the commonality of share human experience. Indeed, human empathy is so powerful that the government works hard to conceal its most barbarous acts. If the television cameras were admitted to immigrant detention centres, if conditions could be witnessed and individual stories heard, the entire debate about immigration would have a different flavour.

Similarly, although opinion polls in Britain consistently show support for the return of the death penalty, if a British person is on death row in the United States, China or elsewhere there is often a powerful reaction relating to the specific case. It is statistically highly likely that a person condemned to death almost anywhere in the world – not excluding the United States – has suffered one, some or all of: mental illness; child abuse; poor representation; a poor, inappropriate or damaging police and/or judicial process (this list is far from exhaustive): and when the story is heard it is natural to empathise. Everybody has a particular identity and set of circumstances which, when known, place a value on their life that it would not bear if viewed in generalised policy terms. It is the personal, individual story to which people relate, when they have a connection. A connection as insubstantial as a shared nationality may well be sufficient for the individual story to be drawn out.

Human experience suggests that an asylum seeker – or even a proven murderer – has a personal story worthy of attention, but in the public arena of politics this is crowded out by the generalised view. In the case of immigrants, people often assert that they take jobs away from the existing population and depress wages by working for less. True or not – and the reality is rarely straightforward – it sounds like a plausible scenario and appeals to a sense of fairness to which people hold dear. No experience is needed to hold this opinion with conviction; indeed, at the level of public opinion the idea is strong enough to over-ride personal experience. A concern that immigration causes unemployment may easily co-exist with a sense of relief at finding a reliable plumber from Poland, when all the local tradespeople are too busy to fix a tap.

Crime levels have been falling in Britain for years, but people persist in sharing a public belief that the situation is getting worse. Survey respondents may even report reduced crime in their area (based on personal experience) while holding to a "public opinion" that crime is on the rise. This is not because they are stupid or unthinking, but reflects two different processes of the mind, designed to achieve different things. The first one is problem-solving, the second is social interaction. Problem-solving draws on specific experience and the information that a person would require if they were tasked with achieving an outcome. Accurate information is essential for this, whereas the mental processes engaged in social interaction call for a more generalised approach, in which views, opinions and a sense of shared identity all coincide.

Humanity has evolved its problem-solving and social capacities because both are useful. One provides the intellectual tools to work and produce results, the other facilitates co-operation, which allows people to work and solve problems together, producing better results. What happens, however, when the problem-solving process is applied to social interaction, and the social process is applied to solving practical problems? The result is found in modern democratic politics, where all of a politician's problem-solving ingenuity is invested in the social process of staying in power. The real problem-solving work of policy-making must pass through this social, opinion-based filter, which prevents it from addressing actual problems in an effective way.

Colonel Fitzwilliam has a bit-part in this process. He lives in a village a few miles out of town, to which he hurries home for a late breakfast having bought his newspaper. After breakfast he takes his spaniels for a walk, where he finds himself increasingly irritated by the number of cars and the speed at which they travel past him. Naturally enough, he wants slow traffic while he's walking and to be able to drive quickly when he's hurrying home. He shares, therefore, with his neighbours a "social" view that traffic in the village goes too fast, while both he himself and his neighbours drive at the speed they consider appropriate for the conditions they encounter.

Here are two aspects of a single reality. Thirty miles per hour seems fast when you are crushed against the side of the road with your dogs, and slow when you are behind the wheel on an empty road. There is no right or wrong about this, and the only solution is to be aware and considerate. People should drive carefully through country lanes, and should slow right down when they encounter pedestrians (with or without dogs). They should choose their speed sensibly for the time of day and the conditions. Maybe a sign, warning of the likely presence of walkers, would help.

The preceding short paragraph contains, if people will heed it, practical solutions to satisfy the needs of drivers and walkers in many circumstances. It recognises that people are able to exercise their freedoms thoughtfully, out of their human will. The only authority asserted is moral authority, of the sort that people must find in themselves. What it does not say is what should happen if people do not heed this good advice. One cannot force people to want to act well: the force blunts the wanting, even when it exacts compliance. The best that can be attempted is to impede or punish bad actions, but the effect of this, as the colonel discovered when he got stuck in that queue at the bank, is to impede and punish many other people whose goodwill is perfectly sound. In a technological world, law enforcement is increasingly indiscriminate; an effective process of moral engagement, however, requires discrimination as its first ingredient. If the object is to improve behaviour, the reason why people do things should be the first consideration.

For a politician, this is not an easy proposition to make. Just as pharmaceutical medicine has projected the assumption that there is a pill for every ailment, so high spending, interventionist government has encouraged the expectation of a law for every social ill. In this case the villagers (or a vociferous group of them, including the colonel) have decided what they want, which is a lower speed limit and all the paraphernalia of enforcement that comes with it. Any politician struggling to convey the complexities of a counter-argument will soon find that a rival has stolen in and given the answer people wish to hear. They will be happy, at least for a while, when they see the signs and cameras. Rules, regulations and laws are the gold standard of politics because they have the capacity to respond so quickly to public opinion. They create a class of rule-breaking "others", such as those careless or selfish drivers that no known motorist will admit to being; or the drug addicts, benefit cheats, scroungers, louts, tearaway teenagers and drunken hooligans that are no honest voter's son or daughter.

These "other people" are central to political process. At the point at which policies are aired, votes are solicited and new laws proposed and passed, the target is always this remote and unspecified group who are responsible for society's ills. Their defining characteristic is that they are not "us", the people who are advocating or who expect to benefit from a particular proposal. Nobody thinks of themselves as a bad driver, or their son as a shop-lifter, or their daughter as a drug user, when laws and punishments are proposed to control such behaviours. Miscreants are faceless unknowns, who may safely be targeted since no voter is supposed to identify with them. It would require rare courage in a politician to tell Colonel Fitzwilliam and his neighbours that those causing the problem are actually "you, you, and you". This is something they will only discover when the speeding fines start to drop through their letterboxes.

RULES INTENDED TO target "other people" rebound upon society because the more specific they are in their object (the thing that they require), the more generalised they are in their subject (the circumstances in which they are applied). A red traffic light is *objectively* highly specific: it just means "stop" with no room for interpretation. As such, however, it ignores the *subjective* circumstances: whether, in the specific case, there is any actual reason to do so. Hore-Belisha, when Minister of Transport in the 1930s, reduced pedestrian casualty rates at crossings by introducing the orange flashing beacons that bear his name, but drivers still only had to stop if a pedestrian was waiting. A flashing orange light is information whereas a red light is an instruction: newer crossings insist that drivers stop, even when no one is about. At night, cars are often seen waiting pointlessly at empty junctions for the lights to change.

The post-war era has seen a steady increase in the regulatory environment and a drive towards objectification in many areas of domestic law. The legal term for this is "strict liability", which ignores motive and intent. It developed as a way of protecting people who buy faulty goods, making manufacturers *strictly liable* to compensate the consumer, even if they had not been negligent. This is helpful because the consumer avoids the need to dissect the supply chain in pursuit of whoever is truly at fault. Governments, too, have been attracted to this reduction in workload; having so many laws, rules and regulations to enforce, they have appropriated strict liability to the point that it is increasingly the norm for regulatory frameworks.

The danger of this approach is that normal, sensible, considerate behaviour may become illegal. In 2009 two policewomen were reportedly stopped from looking after each other's children on alternate days. The exchange was deemed to be remuneration, and both were required to register and function as paid childminders, conforming to and being inspected on a set of standards laid down by Ofsted (the inspection authority). The good intention is palpable in these official-sounding words, and yet the road to perdition is paved with this sort of thing. There was no conceivable objection to the behaviour of the women, but a legal tripwire had been triggered, meaning that this normal, reasonable, even laudable, behaviour was not allowed to continue.[1]

Rules that prevent people from applying their own reasonable moral judgements to guide their behaviour may also insulate them from the obligation to do so. The sheer complexity of tax rules accreted over generations turns tax-reduction into a game in which there is no "right amount" to pay. Depending upon how determinedly the rules are interrogated, one may pay a great deal or very little, and wealthier people have greater scope for deploying the resources required to help them minimise their payment in accordance with the rules. No one should be surprised, therefore, that people lacking such resources resort to cash transactions, selective amnesia and gen-

---

1   Susbequent rule changes appear now to allow this specific arrangement.

erous approximations to achieve an equivalent (even morally equivalent) outcome. Rules can easily create a moral vacuum in which any
arrangement that does not actually break them is considered acceptable, and people operating in this vacuum invariably push the rules
to their limits. The general rule of taxation appears to be to pay as
little as possible, so even a little dishonesty may be acceptable if it
achieves what could, in the hands of an expert, have been achieved
by legitimate means.

Within human relationships, people can tell what the rules are
designed to achieve. If a cricketer grazes the ball with the bat and
is caught, he knows he is out, even if the umpire does not see the
slight contact between leather and willow. Whether he "walks" (i.e.
gives himself out) is actually less relevant than whether he knows;
the opportunity to behave well is a human gift of which people
may not always avail themselves. In village cricket the player usually "walks", but the commercialisation of the game has tended to a
stricter application of the rule at a higher level. The objective test is
that the player is out, not if they hit the ball, but only if the umpire
decides that they hit the ball. Because high level sport is a business,
the objective regulations supersede a player's honesty and goodwill.
Rules often deny people the opportunity to behave well; for those
stuck in a moral limbo such as a complex tax code, "obeying the
rules" not only obstructs morally good behaviour but may just as easily encourage behaviour that is morally wrong.

No more striking example has been seen in recent years than the
parliamentary expenses scandal, which was the biggest political news
story of 2009. When British MPs and peers were found to be playing
their expenses system for personal gain, they fell back on the asser-
tion that their often extravagant claims were entirely "within the
rules" of a system that appeared to have evolved as a back-door way
of supplementing their salaries. Here, splashed over the newspapers
for weeks and weeks, was a vivid lesson in how "obeying the rules"
need not equate to a morally sustainable position. The very weakness of rules, which is their blindness to individual cases, proved
their undoing. Because they could not easily distinguish between

legitimate expenses and self-serving excess, they were not so much "obeyed" as "used" for personal advantage.

Moral judgement; personal responsibility; the capacity to engage with one another on equal terms: these vital human potentialities are like muscles that need to be exercised if they are not to weaken. A surfeit of rules may easily cause people to suspend their judgement, through fear, or mental laziness, or avarice, with the consequence that these moral muscles fall into disuse. This phenomenon is now endemic in the west, where a sense of rule-based entitlement has overwhelmed the innate human spirit of moral participation to the extent that people now keep their real moral judgements to themselves. The result is a sort of group-think or crowd mentality, which individuals are in danger of losing the capacity to question.

The banking crisis that started in 2007 was founded on precisely this human dysfunction; the regulation of banks, in any case rather lax, had no moral basis to sustain it and degenerated into "anything you can get away with". It was the inevitable consequence of the shift from a culture of moral probity that was so essential to small, diverse City partnerships trading on trust to the formal, institutionalised regulation that accompanied their merger into single, amorphous, shareholder-owned institutions. When probity ruled, someone might cheat but others would take note and the damage could be limited. By undermining individual responsibility in favour of whatever the rules dictate, formal regulation allows people to "park" integrity in their professional lives, effectively washing their hands of the moral consequences of their actions.

WHEN THE PAVEMENTS ARE crowded, people find their path naturally, rarely bump in to one another and are generally tolerant when they do. Sometimes a person is intolerant and pushy, but people cope with this, too. They know that behaviour is rarely perfect and the deal with it, adjusting to the change in circumstances and finding a "workaround" that will get them by. In practice, most of life is like this, having little use for the arbitrary rules that direct it to be led under a blanket of protection from an unidentified and largely imaginary world of hostile "others". At the court of public opinion, however, where politicians reign, a classic exercise in "divide and rule" is carried on systematically, whereby objective rules drawn up to give expression to people's general opinions end up obstructing the subjective desires and intentions to which those same people legitimately hold.

A successful business could never operate in this way. Rather than seeking to obstruct people's subjective wants by imposing an objective framework, businesses create a suggestive framework, which they then ceaselessly adjust in response to the subjective information they receive. Supermarkets are the masters at this. They may ask people for their opinions but they would never make the mistake of relying upon what they say. Instead, they pile their shelves with a vast range of choices and then see what people actually buy. The sales data they amass allow them to manage their product range in such a way that the customers will continue to beat a path to their door.

There is nothing generalised about a supermarket's methods. Every transaction constitutes a one-to-one relationship with a customer; in an increasingly complicated and diverse world the onus upon the provider to match the individual's specific want gets greater, not less. Of course, supermarkets routinely seek to manipulate their customers, but they do so in ways that they think they will like, pushing them in a direction that they are willing to go. A similar approach keeps Google in business. It may have billions of internet pages indexed in its databases, but its primary focus is on the algorithm that transforms a user's search term into the specific web page that they want. Generalisation is useless in this context; like the supermarkets, Google is not coy about making suggestions, but it refines them constantly in response to the user's reactions in order to a provide a closer match to the specific need.

These firms know how to connect with people; they know that specific information penetrates much deeper into human understanding, while generalities skate on the surface of a mind that can do nothing with them. Similarly, the sort of generalities that create public opinion do not provide information that can be productively processed. They connect assumption and solution in a single leap that lacks intellectual process. There is nothing in them that can be worked out.

Think of driving a car. This cannot be done in a "general" way. There are generalisations that can be made, such as "she [generally] drives fast", or "he [generally] drives safely", but driving a car still consists of a sequence of quite specific decisions, actions and reactions to the changing circumstances of the moment. This is what people are good at: dealing with the situation in which they find themselves, in the kitchen, in bed, at work, on the road, with friends, solving all the time specific problems about what to eat, how to cook it, when to make love (and how), how to format a document, how to get from A to B, how to comfort someone, how not to upset someone, which film to go to. If the answer doesn't come immediately, people use their ingenuity to develop a work-around – a solution that will do.

Human minds are built for this; humankind did not survive through the honing of the brain for generalised speculation, but through working out solutions to stay alive and prosper. Evolution has selected for the ability to get out of scrapes and fixes – the situations that killed the people whom evolution did not favour – and to make things work. General questions, however, may cause even the greatest minds to falter. Should a health service be free to the user, or paid for? Is conceptual art a valid art form? What is to be done with asylum seekers? Few people have a point of reference for such questions that would allow them to give an answer behind which they can really stand. If forced, most would say "It all depends": it depends on the facts, the details, the actual circumstances. When faced with a specific question, however – "Should this person be given this treatment for free?"; "Do you like this work of art?"; "What is to be done with this asylum seeker?" – all at once people are back on track: they know what to do.

In a wired-up, technologically advanced society such as Britain, the fundamental problems of survival have, for most people, receded. The social, networking, communicating, generalising aspect is becoming more dominant, and the habit of thinking to survive is increasingly channelled into survival-task surrogates. Problem-solving activities such as crosswords, puzzles and brain-teasers; quiz shows and general knowledge contests; physical challenges, including organised games; video and computer simulations, often providing entire virtual worlds filled with challenges that stimulate the innate human capacity to overcome difficulty and succeed: all of these leisure activities provide outlets for human ingenuity and creativity that are insufficiently called upon in people's daily lives.

The implication – that society is not mobilising its human resources effectively – runs parallel with the increase in the transactional economy, in which so much of human activity is unproductive, serving only to distribute and accumulate wealth in ways that favour the already wealthy. The research evidence supports everyday observation in suggesting that people are not as naturally competitive as classical economic theory would have us believe, but behavioural research also has something to say about what they would rather be doing. In particular, it suggests that financial incentives do not motivate people in the way that economists have traditionally assumed. For, although money prizes have been shown in experiments to accelerate boring, repetitive tasks, they caused people to perform less well in work that required creative thinking. People also performed better in a voluntary task than when they were paid. Pay locates people in a marketplace where differentials cause them to work as hard as the level of pay would seem to justify. If the pay is too low they may decline to work at all. The relationship of master and servant may also absolve them from a sense of responsibility for the outcome of their work. There is no market, however, for voluntary work. Whether helping someone out or performing a social or public good, working for free brings its own reward and its own sense of responsibility for outcome. As such, it fosters a positive self-image, whereas low pay has the reverse effect: by placing a low value on the work done it risks damaging the worker's self-esteem.

Autonomy is the key to this. Volunteers may direct their work where they will, and are at low risk of being exploited. They are more able to give attention to improving things and achieving outcomes related to human needs. Here are three elements of self-affirming work that between them far outweigh mere wealth-accumulation as a motivation for people to get out of bed in the morning. First, that the work is worthwhile, in a human and social sense unrelated to exploitative gain; second, that it engages creative problem-solving skills; third, that it allows scope to self-organise. Work, in other words, should be useful, interesting and autonomous if it is to engage people most effectively.[1] In economic terms it is only necessary that the outcome of people's work should be sufficient to meet their reasonable needs.

THAT EXPERIMENTS SHOULD be necessary to demonstrate that people feel better off and do better things when able freely to exercise their problem-solving and social skills, indicates the extent to which generalised ideas about human behaviour and motivation have taken hold. The counter idea – that it would be better if people were told what to do (and only did what they were told) while engaged in unproductive work that makes other people richer, paying good money to seek the interest and purpose lacking in their real lives through virtual-reality worlds owned by large corporations – does not sound like the sort of thing that would play well on election night. Nonetheless, politics has so lost touch with the centrality of autonomy to the quality of human experience that it is now largely directed to achieving this latter vision.

Because of this, it is not surprising that a dissonance should appear between statistical measures and the human account of aspects of experience. If the fall in the level of crime across the western world in recent years has not registered politically, with people more anxious than before and believing crime to be rising, it could be more closely connected to a broader feeling of vulnerability – and powerlessness to do anything about it – than to the actual level of recorded offences. After all, there are only two categories of societal problem: one is "violence", or threat to the person, whether physical, emotional or intellectual; the other is "poverty", or insufficient access to the things

---

1   Daniel Pink, in *Drive* (Canongate, 2010) has "autonomy, mastery, and purpose." *Drive* contains a useful summary of the experimental research underlying this conclusion.

that satisfy human emotional and material needs. The distinction between these is less than clear-cut; both can give rise to vulnerability not directly from victimhood but from alienation – a sense of living in a world in which things may happen to people over which they have no personal control.

Building and mending relationships, bringing up and educating children, caring for the sick, the infirm, the dispossessed and each other: these are activities central to the human condition, things that people do well if society will only create the conditions that will let them. Any yet the tendency of government in the west has been towards technologising and industrialising them on a scale that is extra-human; people participate in them as directed agents of the state, which overrides their individual human capacity and sense of purpose.

Schools have become education factories, often of a thousand or more pupils, focused almost entirely upon quantitative metrics; prisons are crammed with offenders, their offences often petty and their sentences short, many afflicted with mental illness and backgrounds of appalling deprivation, who come and go through a revolving door of hopelessness; hospitals grow in size and complexity, while the healing capacity of human empathy is lost sight of; the elderly are shuffled off into care homes, to live out their last years as "somebody else's problem" in environments from which regular, empathetic human contact has often been priced out by their corporate owners. Work is focused upon achieving economic metrics unrelated to anyone's sense of purpose or wellbeing. In so many situations, people are struggling against the grain of government policy to make human connections – or else, increasingly, are giving up on the attempt and closing their minds to the human consequences. These are not developments that anyone intended or wanted; they have come about through nothing more devastating that a failure of political imagination – the imagination required to connect politics to the capacity of the human will. The urgent task of politics is to recover that imagination, and so create the conditions in which people can undertake the fundamental tasks of human relationship for themselves.

Chapter 8

HUMAN VALUE

...and how to measure it

WHOSE WORK IS more rewarding? The person who cleans the male toilets at Paddington Station, or a surgeon working at the nearby St. Mary's Hospital? Economists would say the latter. Apart from being better paid, a surgeon has studied hard for and chosen their field whereas a toilet attendant is probably only doing it for the money. Buried in there somewhere is a tacit assumption that a toilet attendant would rather be doing something else, whereas a surgeon might not be.

The reality may be rather different. "Rewarding" is not just about pay; it involves people feeling good about their work, which in turn connects with the benefit that society gains from what they do. If *useful, interesting and autonomous* are the criteria applied, The job of looking after the toilets at a busy London railway terminal may score quite highly. It offers plenty of scope for self-organisation, which allows a person to feel pride in their work. It is clearly useful, and it calls upon some problem-solving and people management skills. On the fourth criterion, however, that work should afford people enough wealth to support a reasonable standard of living, it is likely to score much less highly. So-called "menial" tasks of this nature are significantly undervalued in sophisticated, high-tech economies.

A surgeon may also feel undervalued, but probably not because they struggle to get by on their pay. Although their work appears to be both useful and interesting, it may be much less of both that it could be. This depends on how it is organised, which is largely out of the surgeon's control. Frustration at the organisation of work is endemic in Britain's health service; too much of the surgeon's prob-lem-solving energy may be spend in negotiating the management system that controls how they work, with the result that they do less good than they are capable of. Work that could be highly rewarding may send people home worn out and demotivated every evening, their positivity undermined by stress and anxiety, triggered by the incapacity to function to full effect.

The quality of work depends on how people experience it, just as the quality of wealth depends upon the use that they make of it. Toilet cleaning may be rewarding, if well organised; open-heart surgery may be less so, if organised poorly. Social organisation is central to the experience of work and the quality of output, so gov-ernment has a role facilitating people to work in the most rewarding way both for them and society. Above all, this means producing the wealth that people want and need, which includes not only clean toi-lets and mended bodies but the wealth that people derive from their personal and social lives. Part of the government's facilitating remit is to ensure that both toilet attendant and surgeon have ample time outside their paid employment for the social interactions and self-development essential for a healthy and fulfilling life.

Facilitating means making happen more easily the things that peo-ple either do or would like to do for themselves, or would like to have happen. So a facilitating remit requires that the government not make judgements that people can more effectively make for themselves. Foremost of these is deciding what to do with their lives, which includes deciding how their work, and the wealth it produces, is valued. The basis of measurement must be the one that people would use for themselves, reflecting the human rather than the mar-ket value of things. Those clean toilets, for example, are assessed by the market at 30 pence for each person having a sufficiently pressing need to be willing to pay to make use of them. At 10,000 people a week, the market value is £3,000, which is factored into the calcula-tion of national GDP. No human being, however, would choose to think in such terms. The human value does not lie in the 30 pence, but in the relief gained from using a toilet, and particularly one that is clean. If the toilets were free to use, more people might do so, in which case the human value would increase while the market value reduced to zero.

People value the cleaning of toilets not by price, but for the human benefit that a clean toilet brings. That is why they clean them in their own homes, without expecting cash payment. This indicates that *how* people pay for things makes a difference to human value. The transactional sum requested to use a public toilet may seem arbitrary and off-putting, but the alternative of "free to use" in money terms does not mean free of human effort. At home, as in public, toilets do not clean themselves. In both cases people expect to earn the benefit with their work, either collectively, through their contribution to the work of society, which circulates through the economy using money as a medium of exchange to enable a nominated cleaner to take on the task, or directly, scrubbing away themselves without the intervention of money at all. In neither case do people quantify their contribution, and nor would they choose to. They are much less inclined to count their input than simply to appreciate the result.

Surgery is the same. However greatly people value having their bodies repaired, it does not come easily to quantify that value in money terms. Although the extent and complexity of operations varies greatly, no one would place a lower value on a life saved just because the operation happened to be a simple one. Indeed, placing a monetary value on surgery becomes almost nonsensical when one appreciates that *not needing* surgery has value, too. If being cured of heart disease is worth something, logic suggests that a life untroubled by cardiac problems is worth even more.

In health, as in so many areas of human experience, market value is a poor approximation to human value, even when, superficially, they appear to coincide. Activities that cause heart disease, such as smoking, drinking and eating junk food, have undoubted market value, adding value to the national economy just as the money spent on the resulting heart surgery contributes still further to the national accounts. They also have a human value that may compensate for the harm they cause when people do them for pleasure. Often, however, people smoke or drink to relieve workplace or domestic stress, while others eat junk food because it is cheap and filling. Assuming that people truly able to choose would prefer a healthy life to one plagued by illness and the need for medical intervention, it follows that human value is also attached to eating less, and more healthily, and drinking and smoking as little as possible. Walking, (which is free), has a value in this context that driving (which is expensive) does not, even though driving adds far more value to the national economy. Even the exercise gained from regular housework (including cleaning toilets) is said to lead to a longer and healthier life.

The price in money terms of human activity has no clear correlation with human benefit; good or bad things may be equally expensive, while some of the best things in life cost no money at all. A person who pays a subscription to a dating agency does not forever value a resulting relationship in terms of that sum; a person who swims regularly in the sea does not value their fitness less than somebody who pays for a personal trainer. A private education may or may not be better than one supplied free by the state, but knowing the date of the Battle of Hastings is not more or less valuable just because the acquisition of that knowledge has been paid for.

Social and personal wealth, such as friendship, knowledge and good health, are not necessarily free in money terms; but, like clean toilets, they share the common feature of human as opposed to monetary wealth – their value is measured in outcomes rather than prior inputs. An input of 30 pence gives rise to an empty bladder. The value in classical economics resides in the 30 pence, whereas the human value resides in the comfort of the empty bladder. An input of £100 to a dating agency has as its outcome a life-long partnership or marriage... the point hardly needs to be laboured: when things have human value, people appreciate them for what they are, not for what, if anything, they pay to get them. This principle also applies to material products. Wine is commonly bought on price; instead of necessarily buying the cheapest, people pay a sum that reflects the quality they are after. The association, however, between price and value tends to disappear when the bottle is opened. The price as a determinant of value does not outlive the enjoyment or disappointment when the wine is consumed.

The value of many consumer products follows this pattern. The experience of ownership or consumption, whether good or bad, rapidly displaces the purchase price as the arbiter of worth. Are the advanced features of a smart phone "worth" anything to a user only dimly aware of their existence and with no interest in making them work? For how long do brands uphold the value suggested by their premium price, compared to similar products of nondescript provenance? The whole question of price, indeed, turns on an economist's assumption that people pay in accordance with their choices. In reality, as retailers know, price sensitivity is highly susceptible to the impressions that marketers and advertisers place in people's minds. Remember those trainers that left an Asian factory for £3 and were sold on a British high street for £80 or more? There is no "right price" for such a product, but simply the accretion of a number of essentially arbitrary margins added by marketers along the length of the supply chain. For the want of any real point of reference for value, people generally pay what they are asked.

Many people enjoy shopping, and the correlation between monetary and human value is certainly strongest at the moment of purchase. Thereafter, it serves little purpose: the value those trainers hold for each purchaser will vary greatly, depending upon how comfortable they are, how "loved", how suitable to the purchaser's activities and how many other pairs of shoes the purchaser owns. It is only when things are bought as investments rather than for use that the link between price and value survives the experience of ownership. Financial instruments exist only in their paper value, but artworks and even houses lose a part of their human value when bought only for financial gain. The storing of wealth in this way destroys rather than creates human value, as we shall see.

THE ECONOMIC CONCEPT of human value, expressing the true worth of goods, services and opportunities rather than their traded value in the market, is something with which economists and politicians are only gradually coming to terms. Behavioural science, and the new field of behavioural economics, in particular, is showing the market to be a poor mirror of human behaviour because people do not operate on the market's terms. The response to the unsurprising discovery that people are "bad" actors in the market place (i.e. not good at pursuing their self-interest) has focused on trying to improve the relationship between people and the market by making the choices more explicit. In Britain, which spearheaded the move towards choice in utility services following the privatisations of the 1980s, regulations have been needed to reduce a bewildering range of tariff options to a smaller and more transparent number of possible deals. The logic of this process takes it one stage further. Since the utility companies know far more about their customers' patterns of consumption than the customers know about the utilities' tariffs, much the best way of giving everybody the best deal is simply that – to oblige the companies to give them the best deal.

Richard Thaler and Cass Sunstein – both self-professed free-marketeers – come close to this conclusion in their book *Nudge*[1], a concept in behavioural engineering that has found political favour in some quarters. Nudges are signals – sometimes overt, sometimes semi-conscious – that push decision-making in a particular direction, encouraging people to respond to market incentives by posing them in specific ways. For example, it has long been known that people's purchasing is influenced by the way in which goods are displayed, and it should be no surprise to anybody that the choices they make in the marketplace are nowhere near as free as classical economists would like to pretend. Left to itself the market will nudge people towards making larger, more expensive purchases in order to increase the transactional profit, but a display might equally be configured to loftier ends, such as nudging people into making healthier choices. Either might suit a government's purpose; the former tends to an increase in turnover and therefore GDP, while the latter saves on healthcare costs.

---

1   Thaler R. and Sunstein C., *Nudge, Improving decisions about health, wealth and happiness*, Yale, 2008

Thaler and Sunstein advocate the enlightened use of this approach but recognise its limitations. They draw attention to the important place of the *default* in a choice-driven society. Little-known before the advent of personal computing, the default is the choice that the machine or system makes for you, unless you decide to change it. Some systems now change their defaults as they learn more about the user, indicating that the machine is on the user's side. Most systems, however, are owned by someone, and that someone is usually an organisation with its own distinctive interests. For a default to be effective in nudging people towards what they truly want, the system needs to be immune to such ulterior motives. It needs both to understand the concept of human value and to recognise it in practice when it sees it.

The way GDP is calculated is a default that fails on all three counts. Because it includes only money-denominated transactions it neither knows nor recognises productive, unpaid activity that is replete with human value. In this respect it is profoundly compromised by commercial interests: we saw in Chapter 6 how powerfully it nudges government to favour transactional over productive activity, since transactional activity causes the turnover of money to increase much faster. The nudge effect radiates out across all the departments and agencies of the state, influencing policy and decision-makers to seek to maximise the sort of activities at which markets excel. As we have seen, markets are highly effective at promoting transactional activity, but also highly *in*efficient at connecting producer and consumer since so much productive value is stripped out on the increasingly tortuous journey between the two.

Efficiency is the ratio of input to desired outcome, which can only be measured if the desired outcome is correctly identified. A bulb that takes 100 watts of electricity to produce 60 watts of light is said to be 60% efficient, assuming that light is wanted rather than heat, which accounts for the 40 watts that are lost. For a government, using market value to measure GDP is the political equivalent of measuring the heat from a light-bulb. A society struggling with economic depression, huge debts, social deprivation, rising inequality, environmental degradation and climate change simply cannot afford to have a default measurement that is so off-target.

GDP ITSELF IS not the enemy of change that it is often made out to be. Conceptually, it is a neutral formulation of what a society produces. The fact that it is expressed in money is no inherent failing. A statistical measure has to be enumerated to be comparable, even if the source data are not precise. Much of the content of GDP calculations is derived from surveys and approximations and even a statistical measure of happiness can be stated as an index, derived from the answers people give to questionnaires. The real use of such indices is comparative: economists and politicians obsess over the percentage difference between each period's measurement because, provided the methodology is consistent, this provides a real picture of progress or regression on the chosen yardstick.

The problem, therefore, is not with GDP itself, but with its status as a sacred cow and with its default means of calculation. That status rests on two pillars, both unsound: first, that the measurement is some sort of absolute, not to be mucked around with, and second, that it is a uniform international yardstick beyond the influence of national governments. Because of its apparent immutability, political effort has been directed not at changing the list of activities that GDP measures but at the development of new, alternative measures more closely aligned with human need. The United Nations has provided a lead; other international organisations and some national governments have taken up the challenge and numerous think tanks, research bodies and pressure groups have joined in.[1] This enthusiasm for alternative indices of human wellbeing, has, however, while challenging GDP philosophically, let it off the hook in practical terms.

It is true that GDP has global resonance; its existence is underpinned by numerous international and inter-governmental arrangements that have limited the room for manoeuvre in this respect. Group-think has gone global, and it will require an act of national

---

1   Fioramonti, L., *Gross Domestic Problem*, London, 2013, has a useful summary.

political courage or international co-operation to change significantly the way in which GDP is measured. Nonetheless, because the way of measuring GDP is selective (driven by choice or circumstance) rather than absolute, its composition can, in principle, be made more useful. Its calculation is the responsibility of individual countries, carried out by statistical agencies on behalf of their governments. The brief that a government gives its statisticians is capable of being changed politically; indeed the basis of GDP calculations is routinely adjusted to reflect structural changes to a national economy. Change, therefore, can be achieved piecemeal, through small adjustments in different countries, whenever the political dynamic allows. Provided the direction of travel is broadly consistent, the change becomes cumulative and may accelerate. When one country benefits, others will be keen to take note.

This, then, must be a key objective of human politics, to change the default calculation of GDP, with the starting point of including unpaid and voluntary work of the sort that is commonly paid for. Its purpose is to nudge the economy towards favouring productive work, to reduce the amount of productive energy that is sucked out of people's lives by transactional activity and ensure that the work they choose to do is properly valued in national policy. Implicit in the proposal are a range of extensions – to devalue transactional work within the GDP calculation; to exclude the trading of financial instruments from the calculation entirely; to exclude the production of weapons and the operation of security apparatus; to offset the loss of natural resources against the value of extracting them to ensure that policy is fully focused on resource conservation. It could even be calibrated to acknowledge that wealth is worth more in the hands of people who really need it than in the bank accounts of people who have plenty already. Once the principle of human value has been introduced, the measurement of GDP can be re-based to favour the production of real wealth, the things that people want and need, over the useless transactional activity with which people's productive and creative lives are now so overwhelmed.

"Unpaid and voluntary work of the sort that is commonly paid for" includes childcare, gardening, cooking, cleaning, the maintenance and repair of houses, cars and belongings, house-building... the list is considerable, but it makes sense in terms of the human value that people create and consume every day. The preparation of a meal from raw ingredients may take longer and require more care than putting a ready meal in a microwave, but, as an alternative to the paid work of the ready-meal factory, it has no less right to be registered in the national accounts. Including unpaid work in the calculation of GDP does not challenge its conceptual framework; anyone can see that the output is the same whether people clean their own windows or pay others to do so, and statisticians are quite capable of placing a value on clean windows and home cooking without cash changing hands. The effect of their doing so, however, would be dramatic. Paid work in a developed economy is increasingly more likely to be transactional, whereas unpaid work is usually productive. Merely by starting to measure unpaid work as part of GDP, government policy would start to favour a shift from transactional work towards the sort of productive economic activity that people can do for themselves and each other. All sorts of additional social benefits may then flow, in the form of the physical, mental and emotional health that people derive from engaging is autonomous, engaging and productive work.

GDP calculated on this basis is not a complete measure of human value. It still does not measure the relief of an empty bladder, or the value of a body that does not require surgical repair, but it nudges strongly in the direction of policy changes that ascribe value to positive human experiences over transactions of mere monetary worth. Indeed, it makes possible human value-based policies that challenge the current, profits-driven economic culture at its very roots, as we shall see in the following chapters.

Chapter 9

THE COST OF LAND

...and the value of shared commons

"AN ENGLISHMAN'S HOME is his castle", agreed the great jurist Sir Edward Coke[1] in the 17th century. But what it cannot be is a castle in the air. In English law it is the land, not the structure built upon it, to which a right of occupation may be granted, which is why the purchase of a house is confirmed by completion of a *land transfer*. The house merely comes with the land, along with anything else that happens to be fixed to it.

To the residents of the top floor flat in a tower block, that interest in land, shared among so many, may seem less important than the condition of the roof above their heads. The building, after all, has a function: to provide, as Le Corbusier put it, "machines for living in", in which roof, walls, doors and windows create a secure container for people and their possessions, while mechanical light, heat and cooling create a comfortable environment in which activities such as socialising, cooking and sleeping can be carried out undisturbed. Among the great French modernist's own castles were massive municipal blocks containing hundreds of homes – so-called *unités d'habitation* into which communal facilities were also integrated. With these schemes he sought to nudge the idea of "home" towards a wider social engagement, making a virtue of high density living and acknowledging the land as just another finite input, like concrete, steel and glass.

---

1   "For a man's house is his castle, et domus sua cuique est tutissimum refugium" [and each man's home is his safest refuge]. *The Institutes of the Laws of England*, 1628

Is a house a machine for living in, or is it an interest in land? The market thinks it has the answer, for it places a far higher premium on location than on structure. It is true that a poor house in a good location may be improved or rebuild, and many a speculative fortune has been made in this way. The reverse is much harder, for no amount of money can make a silk purse out of a house located in a sow's ear. Matching the size and quality of a house to its plot of land is a dark art practised by developers, for whom land, not buildings, is the commodity in which they deal. Developers buy land, divide it up into smaller parcels and sell it on to home-buyers at a profit. The houses they place on those parcels are nothing but a cost in their business model: they seek to build, as cheaply as possible, whatever will maximise the value of each given parcel.

Nobody minds paying for another person's productive work. The work of the trades and craftspeople who make a house is both quantifiable and long-lasting: it is more often repaired or updated than completely replaced, so it holds its value well. The work of bricklayers, plasterers and joiners from centuries ago is still highly-prized. The land that sits beneath a house, however, is not something that anybody has worked to create. People may have worked to prepare it – to clear it, drain it, landscape it, run roads to it – but that is part of the work of construction. The value of the land itself, the right to occupy the little parcel outlined in red on the Land Registry plan, derives entirely from *ownership*, a concept that has evolved considerably over the centuries.

As we saw in Chapter 3, the right to occupy land has been associated through history with a corresponding duty of service to the crown; it was not until the 17th century that English landowners finally broke free from this royal prerogative by asserting the right of parliament to govern. Parliament until well into the 19th century was an assembly of landowners elected by property-owners, since only property-ownership bestowed the right to vote. Throughout the parliamentary period, therefore, the interests of politics and land-ownership have been closely intertwined. Those interests, and the enclosure of common land that so greatly advanced them, unravelled the final remnants of feudalism and placed the market in control, culminating in the "property-owning democracy" of Mrs Thatcher and her successors.

The rights to which landowners were historically so attached concerned the income they could derive from their ownership. Land was only valuable if it could generate marketable produce such as food or fuel, and it is logical that the value of building land should reflect these productive uses. When a farmer decides to build a house on a carrot field, the cost of the land should equate to the value of the loss in the production of carrots, provided no extraneous market forces interfere with the equation. And so it would, more or less, in a truly free market, for there is no shortage of carrot fields and their equivalent if people were permitted to build where they choose. The latest research[1] shows that only 7% of the UK's surface is classified as urban, a figure that includes rural development and roads, car parks, airports, etc. Less than 1% is occupied by flats and houses. The market, however, is most definitely not free; government restrictions on land use are exceedingly tight, permission to build houses is difficult to obtain and the land to which it is granted is not always released freely onto the market. The UK's ten largest house-builders, for example, owned or controlled, in 2012, about 300,000 house plots while selling new dwellings at a rate of about 50,000 a year.[2]

These developers would argue that their well-stocked land-banks, and the high profit margins that they seek, are justified by the uncertainties of the planning process that may leave them holding land in limbo for a number of years. Maintaining the value of their holdings becomes, in these circumstances, a primary concern, and the obvious way for them to do this is to keep the housing market in short supply. In this way they, and other landowners, are both victims and beneficiaries of the politics of land use, for the very difficulty in getting planning permission is what makes the process so profitable on the occasions that it succeeds. It is strongly in the interests of people

---

1   UK National Ecosystem Assessment (2011)
2   By their own account: annual reports and analyst presentations, 2012/13

who own housing land that permission to build on land that they do not own should be hard to come by.

For no group of people is this more true that the millions of small landowners who own or share in the handkerchief of land beneath and surrounding their own home. For these tiny plots, typically less than a tenth of an acre and worth a few hundred pounds at agricultural value, they have paid sums that range from 80% or more of the house price in central London to about 30% on an estate of new houses in the north of England. Whether in the hundreds of thousands, or mere tens of thousands of pounds, these sums have been invested speculatively in scarcity value, with the success of the speculation dependent upon housing land remaining in short supply. On average, since the 1970s, this has paid off handsomely, attracting ever larger numbers of people into buying houses and flats purely for speculative purposes. In the boom market in London in 2013, 80% of newly built flats were reportedly sold to speculative buyers, many from abroad, intent on letting out their purchases as they watch their capital value accumulate.

Having bought scarcity, house owners have no interest in seeing its value eroded by an increase in supply. They are similarly averse to development that may affect the context and amenity value of their property, restricting their views and their privacy while crowding their streets with additional vehicles. This so-called "nimby-ism"[1], entirely rational from a self-interested point of view, reinforces the place of politics at the heart of planning decisions and who should profit by them. The connection between landownership and political influence is as intimate today as it has ever been in history, the only difference being that a substantial majority of British households are now members of the landowning class. Their power is such at the ballot box that there is a strong case for saying that the shortage and high price of building land has much less to do with efficient use of resources than it does with the interests that combine to keep house prices high, and rising.

---

1   Not In My Back Yard.

Government intervention in the UK housing market is nothing new. It dates back at least as far as the rent controls that were introduced in 1915. Since then, policy has variously favoured both home ownership and the rental market, focusing on affordable rented housing in the immediate post-war period and subsequently on home-buyer incentives such as the right to buy for social tenants and the long-running MIRAS scheme that gave tax relief on mortgage interest payments. The accidental creation of a perverse political incentive not to meet the rising demand for housing was a consequence of the paradigm shift that occurred when home ownership came to be viewed as a long-term investment in its own right, as well as somewhere to live. A range of financing arrangements for house purchase was introduced, applying investment models more appropriate to endowments and pensions than to bricks and mortar. Governments, keen on self-reliance and wishing to encourage people to save for their futures, saw house ownership as a way of advancing this. In the 1980s, when the vision of a property-owning democracy was coming into focus, new incentives to purchase were introduced and home-ownership increased at it fastest-ever rate.

The fallout from this speculative surge is illustrated in the graph below. The solid line shows, using the left hand scale, the ratio between average gross household earnings and average house prices. Ironing out the peaks and troughs it is clear that, from 1961 until the late 1990s, house prices increased gradually from about three to about four times average earnings. Much of this increase is attributable to the higher quality of the millions of new homes being built. As people got wealthier, they were able and willing to spend more on their houses, which now had central heating, fitted kitchens and multiple bathrooms. From 1998, however, there is a dramatic fall in affordability, with the ratio of house prices to earnings doubling to nearly eight times in the period to 2010[1].

---

1 The figure used for house prices is the average "simple" price, i.e. the average price at which houses were sold and the amount, therefore, that households had to find to pay for them. Because the quality of houses was improving over this period, this is higher than the "mix-adjusted" figure for average house prices that is often quoted.

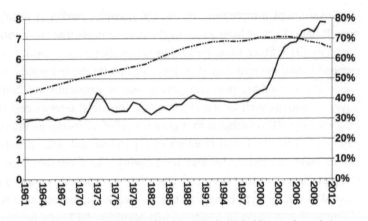

*Average house price as multiple of average household annual earnings
(solid line, left scale); Percentage of households owning their homes (dotted line,
right scale). Source: ONS*

The dotted line in the graph, using the right hand scale, shows the percentage of households that owned their homes over the same period. This rose steadily while prices remained in the range of three to four times earnings; it then peaked at about 71% in 2003 before declining rapidly, losing the previous 15 years growth in just nine years as the ratio of prices to earnings began its steep climb. Nobody can be surprised that the number of home owners should reduce as houses become less affordable; bearing in mind, however, that affordability is primarily an issue for first-time house buyers who are not already invested in the market, this decline in ownership is well set for the longer term. Having been triggered by a rise in house prices to five or six times average earnings, their continued rise to seven or even eight times is certain to accelerate the decline in home-ownership even if affordability stabilises at that level.

What the graph illustrates is a major and rapid change in the underlying certainties of the British housing market. The barrier of affordability that has sustained the market for over 50 years has finally been breached, and with both interest rates and inflation low there is little prospect either that mortgages will become cheaper or that the value of housing debt will succumb to rising wages and prices. The reverse is more likely, since a toxic combination of rising interest rates and falling or stagnant real wages has the potential to place existing mortgage holders into default, adding existing home owners to the swelling ranks of families for whom the first rung on the "housing ladder" is already unachievable. For the market to correct itself in its current form, either house prices must halve or average wages must double, which is the equivalent of saying that the situation will not resolve itself without major structural alterations to the economic system that has brought the housing market to this crisis.

What we are witnessing is the gathering nemesis of the political and economic reforms of the 1980s, which rejected the socially benevolent consensus of the post-war decades in favour of a "free market". So far from being free this was highly controlled, in order to create the conditions for a home-owning democracy in which the homes, ultimately, would be beyond the reach of those who did not already own them. It was a solution that worked only for a single generation, which could buy houses in the '70s and early '80s and watch their values balloon over the next thirty years to ten times the price they paid for them. Since the year 2000, however, the housing market in Britain has lost touch with its function; what seemed a harmless addiction to property prices in the 1980s and early '90s has been revealed in all its toxicity, leaving millions denied the benefits of affordable housing. The children of that golden generation have almost no prospect of buying homes on their own, while their parents, still only in their fifties and sixties, have limited capacity to help them without selling up. Instead, more and more people are forced into a largely unregulated, over-priced and insecure rental market – a market based on speculation in which the opportunities to profit have been concentrated in ever fewer, richer hands.

The nature of that rental market has changed dramatically. In the 30 years before 1981, of nearly ten million dwellings built, over half were social housing, available for long-term, affordable rental; in the 30 years after 1981, fewer than six million dwellings were built, of which fewer that a million were social housing. The number of dwellings built and sold privately in the two periods was almost the same, at about five million, but *four million fewer* social housing units were built in the second period, despite a faster increase in the population and mounting pressure to create more households as families fragment into smaller groups.

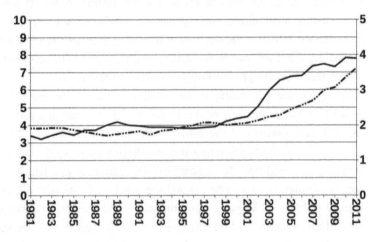

Average house price as multiple of average household annual earnings (solid line, left scale); Number of private rentals, in millions (dotted line, right hand scale).
Source: ONS

Reflecting those figures, the number of social renters peaked in 1981, just before the Thatcher government launched the "right to buy" that saw local authority-owned social housing sold to its tenants at knock-down prices. In the period of sustained growth in owner-occupation to which this contributed, the number of households renting from private landlords reached, in 1988, its lowest level in the 20th century, at 1.7 million. Between 1988 and 2012, however, the numbers renting from private landlords more than doubled, to 3.8 million, and the remarkable thing about it was the pattern of that growth. The first quarter of the increase took 15 years, to 2003; the second quarter took five years; the final two quarters took two years each. From an average of 35,000 a year prior to 2003, the number of *additional* private rentals had increased to 250,000 a year by the end of the period, a rapid acceleration that matches closely the increase in the price of houses relative to household incomes, as the graph shows.

Here is no surprise, either: if people cannot afford to buy a house, they are forced to rent. Meanwhile, however, new houses continued to be built: between 2000 and 2012 two million new dwellings for private sale were completed and sold, and since the number of households owning their own home hardly changed at all during that period it follows that the equivalent of the entire new housing stock was bought by private investors to let out in the rental market. For such capital investors, rising prices provide not a barrier but a strong incentive to buy, since high prices are reflected directly in the rent they can demand. With the private rental market driving both rents and house prices, the problem of housing affordability has transferred from would-be house purchasers to those for whom even renting is unachievable.

IN MANY SOCIETIES, renting a house is far from second best; there is even evidence to suggest that societies do better in which fewer people own their homes. Among the drawbacks of ownership is the transactional burden of buying and selling, of which the cost in time, money and emotional stress encourages people to stay put rather than seek out more productive opportunities in their work and relationships. A further consideration, however, is the cost in land, when prices are high and a disproportionate amount of money is tied up in investments from which no new wealth is generated. The proportion of a house price attributable to the land pays for nobody's work but goes into a form of "cold storage", where it is unavailable either for consumption or productive investment. High and rising land prices are harmful to an economy as a whole, even if they provide myriad opportunities for individual speculation and transactional gain.

Nonetheless, for thirty years at least, high house prices have been viewed as an economic good. Like high share prices, they project a feeling of success and prosperity for their lucky owners, and with 65% of households so heavily invested, declining house prices carry a serious economic and electoral risk. Nowhere else in the economy are the different interests of the "haves" and the "have-nots" so acutely apparent. Up until the moment that a first-time house buyer signs on the dotted line, they would like houses to be cheaper; even before the ink is dry, however, they can scarcely wait for the latest news on rising prices. Property values in Britain have for decades been a national obsession, masking the reality that housing is a scarcely less basic requirement to sustain life than food and fuel and that high housing costs are a major cause of poverty and deprivation. Of the 35% of households in England who rent their accommodation, nearly half in 2012 were in need of government Housing Benefit to make it affordable. These government payments average £5,900 per year, which means that each household in England is contributing over £900 to compensate the poorest fifth of the population for the consequences of a housing market that is skewed towards investment rather than human need[1].

The word "compensate" in that sentence is deliberate, for it asks who is being "subsidised" by the Housing Benefit payments? As the price society pays for the high cost of its housing, this subsidy is not to the people who receive it, but to those who benefit from the high rents and rising house values. With a further million households claiming Housing Benefit in the five years to 2012, and home ownership continuing its decline, the political imperative to underpin house values, which has guided thirty years of land use policy, is at last open to question. Among the vanguard of the no-longer-believers stand not only the politically neglected poor but a much more vociferous and powerful grouping – established, unencumbered home-owners deeply troubled by the housing prospects of the already debt-burdened next generation.

In terms of the "efficiency" beloved of classical economic theory, the housing market does better than most. For although new supply is in the hands of the corporate house-builders, most of the business is with the 26 million or so individuals and couples who own homes

---

1   Sources: English Housing Survey 2011-12, and DWP.

either to live in or to rent out. This diversity of control makes the market less easy to rig or monopolise, so an increase in supply should bring prices down, provided it is sufficient to outpace the increase in demand that would flow from lower prices. The simple way to lower the high cost of housing, therefore, is to make more building land available. The challenge is how to lower prices safely, avoiding the potential withdrawal symptoms of disengaging from the chronic addiction to rising property prices that has the British economy in its grip.

Those symptoms, ranging from the unsecured debt of negative equity to the partial loss of a household's lifetime's savings, is why all governments of recent decades have preferred to feed house prices rather than challenge the addiction. The apparent return to "business as usual" in the housing market of 2013, when state-backed guarantees were introduced for home-buyer debt and both the number of estate agents and the average price of a house broke all records, was greeted with sighs of relief across a political and economic establishment that preferred, with policies such as the bedroom tax, to assign responsibility for housing-related poverty to the people experiencing it, rather than a market driven ever-higher by speculative money. Policy is in a classic bind, where both rising and falling prices have profoundly negative consequences, and the lock upon that bind is the speculative character of land ownership, that requires people to commit such enormous sums to a voracious market.

The key to the lock lies in an alternative, socially-inspired model of land ownership, and for inspiration we might return to that moment when King William I, fresh from his conquest of England, claimed all the land of his new kingdom to himself as the person in whom the state resided. Nobody owned an unencumbered freehold: even the greatest nobles were only "tenants-in-chief", holding their land in return for military and administrative services to the king. This gave him the right to tax the land, and therefore an interest in ensuring that it remained as productive as possible. To measure his entitlement the entire productive capacity of the land of England was recorded in the Domesday Book, which King William commissioned.

Today, the state still controls closely the use to which land may be put. King William would no doubt have appreciated that, but would certainly have been amazed to discover that it does so without gaining from the arrangement. The grant of a planning permission, which is in the gift of the state, can raise the price of an acre of land from £5,000 to well over £500,000. The gift, therefore, is a real and enormous one, straight into the hands of a lucky landowner. Nor does the state's benevolence end at this point, for it also provides the roads and services upon which land value depends. When a new underground line was built in London in the 1990s at huge public expense, it is estimated that the rise in the market value of properties near to the new stations was close to £10 billion, and all without any further investment on landowners' parts.[1]

A new model of land ownership would distinguish between this opportunity value of land, which derives from its location and what may be done with it, and the productive value, which is the value of the work that is done upon it or with it. The opportunity value is retained for society, and only the value of the work done on it is privately owned. A person who turns a piece of scrub-land into a productive carrot field owns the productiveness – the fertility they have introduced with their work – as well as the carrots that they grow. This is something they can sell, of which the price is fairly linked to the value of the work they put in to make the land productive. If they sold the land for some other use, of which the opportunity value was greater, that increase in value would belong to the state.

As with carrots, so with houses. A house builder also works on the land, and is similarly entitled to the value of the work that they do. That value comprises only the "machine for living in" that they construct, while the boost the building gives to the underlying land value belongs to the state. The concept is simple enough, and well established in history and culture: the land, like the air, is a "common" – a shared resource. For any builder, buying land is a large expense, the money for which has to be raised or borrowed in advance of and in

1   Lewis M. and Conaty P., *The Resilience Imperative*, 2012

addition to the money needed for the structure. If the cost of land is taken out of the equation, a builder's resources can go straight into construction and they have no incentive to delay the flow of completed houses on to the market.

If landowners are no longer to profit from the huge increase in value associated with the grant of planning permission, decisions as to which land to build on are substantially de-politicised. The implementation of planning policy is driven by precedent, so granting permission to one person to build in the countryside would, at present, have every rural landowner rubbing their hands. Instead, permissions are hard to get, efforts have to be made to distinguish different sites from each other and, because so much money is at stake, the whole process is open to claims of unfairness and even corruption. Take that money out of the equation and planning policy can be simplified; instead of a battle between a community defending its amenity and a landowner in line for a big win, almost any site could be chosen for its local acceptability.

A further key objective of human politics, therefore, must be to isolate the investment value of land and place it in a common-holder fund, where it can be used to benefit society collectively. Various detailed mechanisms have been proposed for this: in all cases the central objectives are to reduce the grip of landowner interest on the supply of new development and ensure that society benefits directly and collectively from political decisions about the way that land is used. The common ownership of land's opportunity value is not a denial of individual property rights so much as a relocation of those rights where they properly belong, in the hands of the producer, limited to the value of the productive work that the producer applies. The retention of the opportunity value by the state is merely a mechanism for preventing other people from monopolising that value at a cost to the producer, thereby profiting from the productive work that other people do.

The legitimate function of the state in relation to land is to ensure that its use is distributed as productively as possible, where productivity embraces everything that people want and need, from food and housing to the pleasure to be derived from landscape, views and the great outdoors. If all the land were held in common, and only the value of the work done upon it (such as building) could be privately owned, people's mortgage payments would be cut in half and far more of their productive wealth directed where it should be, towards those things that they want and need to enable them to flourish.

Chapter 10

HUMAN COMPANIES

Rethinking the corporate state

REMEMBER ALAM, FROM Chapter 2? He was a farmer in ancient Mesopotamia who stock-piled more grain than he needed to get his family through the year. He used the surplus as capital to buy timber, transporting it down from the forest and storing it to sell to his neighbours over time, thus becoming the world's first builders' merchant. Trade of this sort requires capital, because the work of producing, transporting and storing the goods comes long before any payment is received. It also carries the risk of loss, both of the goods themselves as they make their journey and the value of them once they have been paid for. Alam may have a yard-full of timber from far away, but what if someone discovers a new source much closer (and cheaper)? People who invest their capital must be prepared for losses as well as gains.

The value of Alam's capital, and of his willingness to risk it, are key issues in the structure of a modern economy. People want a return on the money they invest; the amount they will accept depends upon their assessment of the risk, which in turn depends upon the quality of a business plan and the people who are going to execute it. Overall, the return on a successful investment has to be big enough to compensate for all the ones that go bad.

Suppose the investment is £1m. The venture is high risk, but the owners of the capital are hoping for 30% a year, or to double their money over three years, if the risk pays off. It does: the hoped-for return of £300,000 a year materialises and after three years the company's shares are offered on the open market. Since the business is now proven, the risk is much less than it was, so new investors are willing to buy the shares at a 10% return, which values the company at £3m. Over the next three years the business continues predictably, turning out a £300,000 profit every year. After six years the perception of risk has diminished still further, the required return has declined to 3% and the company is valued at £10m.

That original investment has seen a ten-fold increase in capital value over six years; the three-year investors have seen a more than three-fold increase. These capital increases have occurred because shareholders are still making £300,000 per year from the company. The amount originally invested, however, and the only amount that the business itself has ever seen, is that £1m of risk capital. Since the risk profile now justifies a mere 3%, the amount paid out on that original investment should drop to £30,000 per year, which means that an excess £270,000 per year is being paid to investors out of the work of the people whom the company employs. Their earnings have not changed; they are stuck with an arrangement that hands over to the investors, in perpetuity, all of the success that has flowed from their productive work. Some of the employees may also be shareholders, but most are not.

The original investors took £900,000 of profits, then sold out for £3m, averaging a 97% annual return over three years. The second group did almost as well: they laid out £3m, took £900,000 of profits and sold out for £10m, averaging an 88% annual return over three years. This example is simplified, because a new business will generally accelerate into growth rather than run steady from a standing start, but the principle is sound. As companies grow in value, their productive workers are expected to transfer wealth to the investors not as a proportion of the amount of capital invested, but as a proportion of whatever valuation of the business the market decides. In this case, the investors justified their continuing return of £300,000 per year in circumstances of minimal risk by valuing the business at £10m, which disguised the 30% return on actual capital invested as a modest 3% dividend. The result is that £9m of surplus wealth is tied up in share values, where, like money tied up in land values, it has no productive use. A further £270,000 is being paid to investors as a return on that £9m, which could be in the hands of workers and consumers, improving the quality of their lives.

When a company's shares are freely traded, the majority of investor capital is directed not towards creating new productive activity but to piggy-backing on the existing capital, taking the profits it generates and pushing up the market value of existing shares. There is still a risk in this, because the values of shares can fall as well as rise, but this is speculative rather than productive risk, because the fluctuations do not affect the actual working capital invested. This is why, for most publicly listed companies, the share price is generally much greater that the sum of capital that has been invested in the business. As a company's shares rise, they suck in more capital, but this wealth stays with investors and is not available for productive use.

INCORPORATION PROVIDES A legal framework to protect investors from management failure or fraud. The political class that created it in the mid 19th century was a small, wealthy elite that knew little of commerce and disdained its practices, while recognising its growing power. It sought to be protected from the consequences of its own ignorance while enjoying the higher returns that could be derived from commercial investment. Thus, inequality was built in to the corporate structure from the outset. The imbalance of power between the investing and the producing classes reflected the extreme social stratification of the time, in which the producing class had no access to political process because its members had no votes. Small wonder, therefore, that the new corporate framework took so little account of the wider social purpose of investment.

A greater wonder is why it still does not. Through the extension of the suffrage in the 20th century producers have acquired a political voice, and more broadly-based social objectives are now so firmly embedded in the political debate that the rights, interests and supposed opinions of "ordinary working people" are routinely referenced as the gold-standard for political parties of all persuasions. Despite this, however, the framework set down in the Joint Stock

Companies Act of 1844 and the Limited Liability Act of the following decade remains unchanged in its essentials, and the shareholder company model remains unchallenged as the standard vehicle for business investment across the globe. The power of capital has been surrendered reluctantly, if at all; an intermediate, dependent class of salaried managers has emerged to defend investor interests, and the role of wealth-producers – even the real wealth they produce – is now a mere ancillary to the objective of securing and maximising a financial return.

A body of company law that was framed to meet the social assumptions of the mid-19th century makes almost no provision for the interests of collaborative producers and consumers. As such, it contributes greatly to the chronic inefficiency of modern economies when converting productive work into human value in which all can share. It gives shareholder companies a strong incentive to prioritise transactional over productive activity, while perpetuating investor privilege by treating the pay of producers merely as a cost on investor return. A more contemporary model, directed at productive collaboration to maximise human value, would reverse this analysis, identifying the price of capital as a cost on productive work. That cost is so high because the share capital of companies provides a highly effective store of inactive wealth.

Responsibility for this lies on both sides of an adversarial political system. The defenders of capital have worked hard to maintain the myth that everyone can share in investment successes – that the cake crumbs falling from the investors' table may become whole slices – provided capital is given free rein. Those speaking for the producers have bought into that myth by accepting the framework and merely arguing for larger crumbs. Thus a long-redundant argument between labour and capital is perpetuated, as if both sides are blind to the new context of a globalised economy in which all the rules and assumptions have changed. So entrenched is this historic confrontation that a collaborative approach based on the production of human value has had little traction. This, however, is the direction in which the corporate model needs to evolve.

COLLABORATION, MEANING "working together", is something more than "co-operation", which means only "functioning together". Pedestrians who avoid colliding on a pavement are co-operating, to allow each other to achieve their different objectives. Collaboration means a shared objective: it allows people to achieve more together than the sum of what each may achieve on their own. When the accumulated wealth of an investor serves the needs of producers through a start-up period in which more wealth is consumed than produced, the relationship may be called collaborative. If, however, the investor proceeds to control all the surplus wealth that is subsequently produced, the relationship shifts from the collaborative to the exploitative. The producers are now paying with their productive work for the opportunity to do the work, which is owned by their shareholder-employers.

People are both producers and consumers. They seek to produce enough to meet their own and their family's consumption, and they collaborate to make that production more efficient, in order to be able to consume more. That "more" includes anything of human value: basic needs such as food and shelter, material goods and the time and opportunity to satisfy emotional, intellectual, creative, physical and social needs, too. The success of a collaboration lies in how much the producers gain as consumers of human value by working together. The shareholder company model undermines this, driving down the value of productive work while seeking higher margins by increasing consumer prices. Producer-consumers and their families (those ordinary working people) are squeezed between low wages and high prices, losing out in terms of human value on both counts.

The objective of human politics must be to prioritise true collaboration in economic activity, to place the production of human value at its centre. This means restructuring the standard corporate model so that investment serves producers rather than the other way round. It means rewriting company law with reference to the social aspirations of the 21st century, making provision for a relationship between investors and producers that maximises the amount of human value produced and available for consumption. It means rethinking capital as a concept – both its purpose and the reasonable expectations that arise from its ownership.

The key to achieve this is to remove the legal privileges of shareholder corporations, in favour of public interest companies prioritising the production of human value. The first step is a restriction of limited liability, to encourage companies that grow beyond a certain size to adopt a public interest stance. Other such privileges are immortality, which allows companies to sustain their wealth from one generation to the next, and corporate personhood, which gives a company the rights of a sentient human being while exempting it from many human responsibilities. The removal of these would rebalance the relationship between companies and individuals, placing companies in an appropriately subordinate role dedicated to the needs, wants and welfare of people.

The principle of a company working in this way is well established, particularly in Britain where the roots of provident, mutual and cooperative business organisations and enlightened entrepreneurship run deep into the 19th century. In the de-regulated business environment that has prevailed since the 1980s, however, public interest companies have struggled to raise investment capital and to compete on price with commercial companies having no institutional commitment to the public good. Many of them assimilated the business practices of their shareholder-owned competitors, leading, through the 1980s and '90s, to a string of de-mutualisations whereby customer-owned businesses (mostly building societies) sold themselves into the commercial market while paying off their erstwhile owners with windfalls of cash.

The ideology of that period, that shareholder gain is the only route to productive efficiency, depends upon measuring output in terms of turnover and success in terms of corporate profits. Thus, successful companies underpay their staff and leave it to government to pick up the bill through a complex system of tax credits and other benefits. Governments accept this, having convinced themselves that companies can only succeed if wages are competitive, terms of employment are flexible and corporate taxation is low. For "competitive" read "inadequate"; for "flexible" read "insecure"; for "low" read "easily avoidable" and a picture emerges of a corporate regulatory environment that has lost all sense of social purpose. In such an environment it is all but impossible for truly social enterprises to thrive.

There is, however, nothing "natural" about a shareholder company, or an economy based on its principles. The mass incorporation of businesses is, in the perspective of history, a recent phenomenon and the legislation that gave rise to it was pragmatic and self-interested rather than principled in its approach. The sacrifice of such pragmatism in favour of ideological deregulation in the 1980s heralded the apotheosis of capital in a corporate economy that knew no boundaries and played out its dramas on a truly global scale, but it also released the seeds of the destruction of authentic productive capacity in many parts of the developed world. The losses suffered by western economies in the face of cheap, imported goods required them to borrow heavily to sustain the rising standard of living to which they had long become accustomed. Well before the banking crisis of 2008, real U.K. wages were in decline[1]; after the crisis hit there was no hiding place, and the inability of governments across Europe and elsewhere to continue papering over the cracks in social expectations became plain for all to see. The old model, designed to suit a mid-19th century patrician class, has finally revealed itself as worn out, and the time long arrived for a new, more productive model of social enterprise to take its place.

PEOPLE ARE NATURAL problem-solvers, and if the problem presented to them in the management of a business enterprise is how to maximise its profits, that is what they will do. There are only two parameters to play with: expenditure on production, which there is constant pressure to reduce, and the value of sales, which must increase. Reducing expenditure means paying people as little as possible, employing as few of them as possible and/or seeking out cheap-

---

1   See Paul Gregg, P. and Machin S., *What a drag: The chilling impact of unemployment on real wages*, Resolution Foundation 2012

er production facilities elsewhere. Increasing sales means finding the optimum balance of sales volume against unit value, to make the overall income as high as possible – i.e. charging consumers as much as the business can get away with.

The true "problem" of a social economy, however, is not that of maximising profits for a small proportion of the already-wealthy, but of producing as much useful human value as possible with as little unnecessary effort or resource, and to distribute it efficiently so that everybody has what they want and need. The technological challenges of production have been largely overcome. Effectively organised, humankind can produce as much as it wants, provided people's natural problem-solving skills are appropriately directed. Changing the rules that govern companies is one simple way of redirecting human capacity, with its desire for work that is "useful, interesting and autonomous" towards a more profoundly collaborative and socially inclusive set of objectives.

In an economy based on human value, people may still gain from entrepreneurship and risk, but because the legal privileges of companies only apply when the underlying objects are socially useful, investor profit is proportionate both to the productive risk and the actual amount of capital laid out. Instead of market capitalisation, dividend payments, or the relationship of share price to earnings, company success is measured in terms of the pay, conditions, working hours, health and education of its producers, the quality of its service to consumers and its capacity to sustain all of these in the longer term. Thus, the purpose of collaborative work is fully embraced in a company's operations: people work in order to create human value that they want and need, and the company exists to assist them in making as much of it as they can.

It follows that a successful company only trades to the extent that this adds real value to its output; that the first object of its production is to squeeze out unnecessary transactional activity, closing the gap between producers and consumers in so far as possible by supplying the producers' own needs directly. Needs such as child-minding, education, healthcare and looking after the elderly – all the care of one another that is central to the human condition, and which is a core component of human value – become, in this context, no longer a cost to be borne but a productive output to be prioritised by a group of people who choose to collaborate. Instead of paying tax, which sends wealth on a long, tortuous and wasteful journey to a central bureaucracy that disburses it back where it came from, a public interest company helps and empowers people to provide traditionally government-funded services to themselves.

Companies that facilitate the creation and distribution of wealth remain the building blocks of an economy, because this is what an economy is supposed to do. Entrepreneurship, considered as the capacity to take on the challenges of creating effective human organisations, remains the key driver for a company to succeed in this way, and innovation remains its most powerful tool. The essential ingredients, therefore, of business, (from *busy-ness*, meaning organised productive activity) are unchanged, but may avoid the transactional impediments that the pursuit of profit places in its path. Apple, Inc. may be one of the world's most innovative companies, but we have seen how few of its resources are directed towards product innovation, let alone social objectives relating to its employees, customers and supply chain. History shows that life-changing innovations in science, agriculture, medicine, transport and even manufacturing have their origins in curiosity and experimental rigour, and the same is likely to be true for socio-economic advancement. The world of shareholder companies is too conservative in this respect; the drive for short-term profit stifles rather than generates true innovation, creating a focus on minor improvements to consumer technology, or new variants of medication for "rich-world" conditions, in pursuit of sales achieved through marketing to envy and anxiety, rather than deeper human need.

Much innovation in recent times has been entirely transactional in its intention. The growth of advertising, and the use it makes of electronic media to drive spending, is one example. Even more profound in its effect has been the rate of innovation in financial instruments in the last twenty years. New methods of packaging investments, calculating their worth and devising markets to deal in them, along with sophisticated computer models for tracking those markets and identifying opportunities for speculative gain, were largely responsible for the banking collapse of 2008. Although neither social media advertising nor the repackaging of financial instruments has any productive purpose, they do illustrate the capacity to innovate in economic relationships, as well as production. Transactional gain exploits such relationships, at a cost both to producer and consumer, but innovation in these areas can also foster positive relationships, creating organisations that bring producer, consumer and the owners of capital into a mutually supportive and beneficial engagement.

The capacity of people to innovate mutually beneficial economic relationships is not in doubt. Such human organisation reflects what people naturally do when they act unconstrained within their families and social networks. Expanding human norms to a scale that goes beyond people's everyday interactions is a matter of opportunity and self-belief, rather than raw capacity. Half the battle lies in acknowledging the possibility of the objective. What then follows is the opportunity to break down the dependent relationship with capital that has served the interests of the wealthy and powerful since the earliest times. Bringing an end to this culture of dependency and replacing it with collaborative autonomy requires that government correct the structural imbalances in society, allowing the emergence of true autonomy as an economic and political force. Those structural imbalances are now global in scale. How they can be tackled at a global level is the subject of the next chapter.

Chapter 11

RUINED BY TRADE?

How rich countries import poverty and poor ones export wealth

PEOPLE LIVE IN nations with national economies, but the rules of those economies are increasingly laid down on a supra-national basis. Not only do companies bestride the globe, shifting wealth across national boundaries to maximise their transactional gains while reducing their tax liabilities, but the way that national economies interact is more and more subject to legally enforceable international agreements, such as those that bind the members of the European Union or the World Trade Organisation. These agreements are based on the premise that trade is necessarily a producer and increaser of wealth, so the global economy has a hard-wired interest in making it as free as possible.

The project, therefore, of forming an economy dedicated not to maximum turnover, or transactional gain, or company profit, but to the production of maximum human value, is difficult to envisage on a national level. Human value includes not just material goods and paid-for services but all the other experiences, opportunities, sensations, thoughts and emotions that make life good to live. A company that acknowledges this, setting its wages and prices to ensure that productive value is distributed in a way that benefits producer/ consumers to the greatest possible extent, is vulnerable to cheap, imported goods made in low-wage parts of the world, that will easily undercut its prices and remove its wealth-producing opportunities. It is rare that its erstwhile customers will spot the trap, will see that by buying cheap, imported goods they are destroying their own prospects of employment, reducing their capacity to create wealth and making themselves dependent upon low-priced imports. It is difficult, also, for a government to legislate to prevent this. Not only are they bound by international treaties but they are condemned by a brief electoral cycle to think in the shortest possible term. In that term, low prices count for a great deal, since they appear to benefit almost everybody.

Nonetheless, a society that allows its own productive capacity to be degraded by cheap, imported goods from parts of the world where wages are much lower is, in effect, importing the poverty of those regions to its own shores by depressing the value of its own productive labour. In doing so it strongly favours investors over producers, feeding a self-perpetuating cycle of rising inequality, which has been a feature of many western economies in the past thirty years. For investors, such trade is highly profitable, since the difference between the low price of imported goods and their sales value goes straight into their pockets. The depressed value of productive labour, however, increases the downward pressure on prices, since rising numbers of poorly paid or unemployed producers are forced to seek out low prices for life's necessities. This, in turn, increases the incentive to investors to source goods ever more cheaply, placing further downward pressure on producer incomes, both at home and abroad.

The decline in demand for productive labour in Britain, as elsewhere in the west, with the consequent reduction in producer incomes, has led to a rise in social deprivation, with incomes so low that many people are unable to live to a standard deemed acceptable by society. The term "acceptable" has particular resonance where children are concerned, to whom governments are committed by international conventions to a minimum standard of care. When incomes are too low, a culture of dependency takes hold, with government expected to undertake the support of families whose needs are otherwise unmet. How it does this is limited by its capacity to tax productive activity. If that activity is absent, or poorly paid, the tax base shrinks, reinforcing a cycle of deprivation, de-motivation and incapacity, which is soon reflected in the poor health, education and other social outcomes that blight generations of unproductive lives.

Importing poverty in this way does little to reduce it for those who make many of the world's consumer products. Although China, in particular, has experienced enormous economic growth on the GDP measure over thirty years, it has done so in the face of rising social inequality and a rapidly widening gap between the rich and the poor, even among the industrialised, urban population. The difference, as ever, is between the transactional gains to be made from controlling the manufacturing and export of low-priced consumer goods, and the persistently low wages of the actual producers. Many of these are migrants from far poorer rural areas, whose limited economic expectations are exploited with excessive working hours, poor conditions and little security. They stand in the first line of vulnerability to the fluctuations in orders and pressure on prices that rich countries seek to impose.

The exploitation of productive workers coming from conditions of extreme poverty is an established feature of large, low wage producer countries in Asia and elsewhere, but it also operates across national boundaries in ways that have much more impact upon western policy. Migration, whether economically motivated or a consequence of political oppression, and whether legally sanctioned or through clandestine channels, is a hot political topic in rich economies where the value of productive labour has been so depressed. For investors, economic migrants are the answer to a problem that, in Britain, sees four million or more people of working age unable to take paid employment and dependent upon government support for their survival. The reasons are a complex inter-meshing of health, aptitude, caring responsibilities and economic viability that renders low-paid work either deeply unmotivating or near-impossible to sustain. A 2006 report[1] commissioned by the government said that employers in what it called "low-skill" areas of work had tried to attract local recruits but that "they were unwilling to take these posts, as often the conditions, pay, hours or nature of the work were unfavourable to them and migrants were more amenable to these conditions".

---

1   *Employers' Use of Migrant Labour,* report by the Institute for Employment Studies for the Home Office, 2006

Migrants are active in roles that are commonly undervalued, such as the hotel and catering industry, seasonal agricultural work, food-processing, construction and care provision for the elderly and infirm. The low wages paid for this work in a rich economy remain attractive to people from countries where incomes and prices are generally much lower. Many are not permanent migrants, but remit a proportion of their earnings back home, where it makes a substantial difference to the lives of their families. They are more than averagely motivated, having shown some determination – and sometimes overcome significant challenges – to get where they are. Many are highly skilled, even if the jobs they take do not necessarily reflect that; indeed, economic migration may be closely associated with economic growth when it brings motivated people to where they are needed. Employers seem to understand this clearly. That government report says that they "cited advantages of migrant workers in terms of their general attitude and work ethic. They tended to be more motivated, reliable and committed than domestic workers. For example, migrants were said to be more likely to: demonstrate lower turnover and absenteeism; be prepared to work longer and flexible hours; be satisfied with their duties and hours of work; and work harder in terms of productivity and speed." The only word missing from that paragraph is "exploitation".

What damages the economic life of a society is not immigration itself, but the way in which low wages exclude local workers, banishing them to a life on state benefits while impoverished migrants are attracted in their place. Here is a second route whereby a rich country imports poverty, paying the newcomers wages that are too low to sustain an acceptable quality of life and thereby undermining the income base of its own people. The resentment this causes against migrants is understandable, but misplaced. Neither the migrants themselves nor those who resent them deserve the abusive characterisations to which they are frequently subject. Both are the victims of an economic system that places personal profit above human need, where producers may only work on investors' terms and where a lack of opportunity to fulfil productive potential is viewed as a social cost (in subsidies and benefits), rather than as an indication of systemic economic failure.

Economic migration, when driven by necessity, is indicative of such failure at both ends of the migrant's journey. The migrant's own country cannot sustain them, while the country of arrival only wants them because they will accept wages that are equally unable to sustain family life in its wealthier economy. That failure arises from losing sight of the purpose of an economy, which is to facilitate the maximum production and effective distribution of human value – all those material and non-material things that sustain and enrich people's lives. An economy structured to engage its own productive population would neither create low-paid vacancies that only migrants will accept, nor oblige its own people to seek work elsewhere.

This principle applies equally to physical trade, the politics of which are less complex and more crudely self-interested than those of migration. Cheap imports are attractive to rich countries when they translate into high transactional margins for investors and low prices for consumers. When, however, they compete with home-produced goods, a political imperative may arise to defend higher prices. Much depends upon the influence of the group affected; Europe and the U.S. both intervene greatly in world markets to protect farm prices, since, although a small part of the economy as measured by GDP, farming remains of high social importance. They do this through a combination of direct subsidy to farmers' incomes, enabling them to sell produce at a lower price than they could otherwise afford, and tariffs levied on imports to increase their price and make them less competitive in the consumer market.

Tariffs levied on goods being imported to a richer from a poorer country are a tax on the poor producers, a direct wealth transfer from the poor to the rich intended partially to offset the poverty imported via free trade and economic migration. International treaty negotiations, such as those that underpin the E.U.'s single market and the World Trade Organisation, aspire to remove tariffs and other barriers in order to increase GDP for all participants. GDP, however, as we have seen, is not a measure of real wealth. It excludes a great deal of the wealth that makes up human value, while including much transactional activity that takes wealth away from true producers. Trade is, by definition, transactional, creating myriad opportunities for such marginal gain. Organisations devoted to maximising its benefits need, therefore, to focus on a different set of parameters reflecting the human value of real wealth production and to apply measures that favour this. A key objective of human politics must be to substitute "trade that is productive of human value" for "free trade" in international treaty negotiations, in order to maximise the production of human value throughout the world.

REMEMBER THOSE TRAINING shoes in Chapter 2? The ones that left a factory in Asia for as little as £3, to be sold on a British high street for £80 or more? They carry a tariff of 16.9% into the E.U., mainly to help producers in southern and eastern Europe, since in Britain the mass-production of clothing and shoes has all but disappeared. Its effect, however, is quite limited. If the trainers land at Felixstowe for £6, including freight, insurance, etc., the duty is about £1, which means nothing relative to the price the consumer will pay. It's small beer to the government, too, for whom VAT on the retail sale will rake in a sum thirteen times as much.

To the people, however, who actually make the shoes and the materials that go into them, that £1 per pair would make a big difference. Returning it to them directly would put some of the benefits of productive work back where it belongs, with the producers, dramatically increasing their quality of life and the human value to which they have access. Such a tariff would operate in a co-operative, rather than a defensive way, both protecting productive activity in the home market and allowing the people in the exporting country to keep more of the wealth arising from their own productive work. More goods will be produced close to where they are wanted, reducing the quantity that are traded and transported merely for transactional gain. Exports will fall but the loss of income to the poorer, exporting country will be offset by the tariff payment. The arrival of that payment in the hands of producers will enable them to consume for themselves the part of their productive capacity that the export market no longer requires.

The effect would be the same if a country placed a tariff on its exports, provided the money raised found its way to the producers. The principle is well established: export tariffs are often used to raise money on a product in which a country is abundant. The English crown in the middle ages taxed exports of raw wool just as its modern successors tax the output of North Sea oil. The purpose then was to fund a string of wars in Europe, but a second outcome was the development of a strong and innovative English textile industry that is sometimes credited with laying the foundations for Britain's subsequent industrial might. More recently, Mozambique taxed the export of raw cashew nuts, in order to give an advantage to local nut processors seeking to add value to the nuts and thereby boost the Mozambican economy. When, in the 1990s, free market economists at the World Bank sought to end the tax as part of a development loan package, the controversy that erupted in academic circles crystallised the issues that divide proponents of monetary GDP growth from advocates of human value. The price paid to farmers for the unprocessed nuts increased, but the local processing industry could no longer compete. If farmers (the poorest and more numerous) had gained at the expense of urbanised industrial workers (poor, but slightly less so, and less numerous), this was considered by some to be a good result. The farmers, however, were now at the mercy of a fluctuating international market in which control is exercised by those who seek a transactional profit.

This case illustrates what happens when collaboration, even if it is not working as well as it should, loses out to free-trade dogma. Like any society, Mozambique is an inter-related, interdependent group of people, whose collective interests are best served by maximising their useful production of human value while minimising transactional loss. Cashew nuts, once processed (shelled, peeled, maybe roasted and seasoned), are much more valuable than when they come from the tree, and much easier to transport, too, without the extra weight and volume. They command a high price in western markets, so a collaborative approach between farmers and processors that takes the finished nuts as directly as possible to the consumers can maximise this value to the benefit of both. If the distribution of that value is imperfect, if the urbanised industrial poor are benefiting at the expense of an even poorer rural population, this is a social problem that need fixing on its own terms by the Mozambican government. Setting the two groups against one another will not achieve it; the relative poverty of two groups is not to be solved by making both, collectively, less well off than they could be if they worked together.

What actually happened when the export tariff started to reduce is also instructive. Prices for the raw nuts did increase, and they were bought up by traders who dispatched them to India, where the cashew industry had developed more processing capacity than its own plantations needed. The fact, however, that traders could pay a higher price for the nuts, *and* pay to convey them in their bulky, unprocessed state across the Indian Ocean for processing, *and* make a profit for themselves, tells its own story. The transactional profit and the additional shipping are both costs to be offset against the real, human value of growing and processing nuts – costs necessarily paid indirectly by the growers and processors, whether or not the latter was carried out in India or Mozambique.

Mozambique is one of the poorest countries in the world, much poorer per capita that India, although in India there is widespread rural poverty, too. So what we are witnessing with this transaction is the export of Mozambique's poverty wages to India, and the import of Indian unemployment (represented by that spare Indian processing capacity), and the poverty that goes with it, back to Mozambique. The transaction was possible because the free market insisted upon by the World Bank made possible an opportunistic trade. That trade created additional GDP, which means that the world ought to feel richer on account of it, but it was actually an exchange of two forms of poverty from which no new human value was created and from which the productive workers have collectively lost out. The only winners were the traders, for whom the coincidence of a lower export tariff in Mozambique and under-occupied (and therefore cheap) nut-processing workers in India presented an opportunity to be exploited.

Cast back two paragraphs, to where it says: "Mozambique is an inter-related, interdependent group of people, whose collective interests are best served by maximising their useful production of human value while minimising transactional loss". To understand the fallacy of free trade, we need to replace the word "Mozambique" in that sentence with the words "the world". Only then can we begin to see that the management of world trade should not be directed at maximising transactional opportunities, however flattering they may be to GDP figures, but at ensuring that trade works efficiently to allows everybody to access what they want and need. This approach will certainly reduce the volume of international trade, but it will increase its usefulness by ensuring that what takes place is both economically necessary (i.e. genuinely wealth-producing) *and* recognises the true value of what is being traded. Getting this value right will reduce the import and export of poverty so that more wealth stays in local economies. This, in turn, will reduce the poverty that forces people into economic migration.

Think of a cheap, imported plastic toy, which, bought for a pound or so, breaks within hours and is thrown away within days. There is such a thing as too cheap: the toy offers hardly any true value while rapidly presenting a problem of disposal. A similar issue arises with many products – from clothing to electronics – which, after a year or so (and often much sooner than that), can be more cheaply replaced than repaired or updated. This cycle of cheap consumption and rapid disposal represents a waste of work that can be avoided if the productive labour is properly valued. If things are worth the true work (including the work of producing the materials) that goes into them, they are also worth the additional work of mending, enhancing or even re-inventing them when their usefulness begins to fade.

To achieve this, the international treaty organisations that govern trade may need to impose tariffs on countries deemed to be importing things too cheaply. There is, however, plenty that individual countries can do for themselves, making creative use both of formal incentives and behaviour-changing nudges to encourage people to seek true value in the items that they purchase. The precedent lies in the fair trade movement, which seeks to acknowledge the true value of a producer's work even if this means that consumers in the west pay a premium for fairly traded goods. Many fair traders are social enterprises, not focused on profits for themselves but on the social usefulness of their activity. They deal directly with producers, reducing the transactional costs between the price the consumer pays and the value received by the producer. Societies have an interest in framing their tax and corporate legal structures to encourage such socially useful business activity, as we saw in Chapter 10.

Nonetheless, even commercial retailers are embracing fair trade, and in doing so they demonstrate that goods are not priced out of western markets when producers are paid an amount for them that more accurately reflects the true value of their work. In truth, the productive workers' share of the retail price of almost any product, whether from a British farm, an equatorial plantation or a far eastern factory, is so small a percentage that the addition of £1 to the price of a pair of trainers, or a few pence to the price of a bunch of bananas or a litre of fresh milk, will, if it reaches them, make a vast difference to the producer without much impact on the viability of the retail operation. A third of all bananas sold in Britain in 2012 were certified as fairly traded, as was 40% of bagged sugar and a quarter of roast and ground retail coffee, according to the fair trade movement. These figures speak for themselves: a combination of consumer pressure and a willingness on the part of the largest retailers to be pro-active has pointed the way to something that would improve the economic health of both rich and poor societies if adopted on a global scale.

To point the way is not to reach the destination, for the deep change that human politics advocates cannot happen in an isolated way, within the context of conventional market forces. Just as rising demand for organic foods, and the constant pressure to increase margins, have created incentives to cut corners with organic standards, so, with fair trade, as volumes increase the focus may shift back from producer value to consumer pricing, rapidly negating the generosity implicit in the fair trade contract. This danger is called commoditisation: it occurs when the "fair-tradedness" of a product has a market value of itself, because people want to buy fairly traded goods. If demand outstrips supply, prices will rise but it will be the intermediaries who benefit, buying from producers at a "fair" price then selling on at an additional profit. If this re-descent into exploitation is to be avoided, and if the global economy is to be rebalanced away from transactional gain towards human value, a concerted effort is needed on the part of consumers, retailers and governments to avoid the marketplace, seeking out producers and delivering the additional value directly into their hands.

Chapter 12

REGAINING PARADISE

Towards a benevolent political economy

THE OBJECT OF human politics is to place the production of human value at the centre of the economic life of society – to optimise not just material goods and paid-for services but all the other experiences, opportunities, sensations, thoughts and emotions that make life good to live. The way that land and land-based production are valued and distributed; the way that collective, collaborative activity is organised to the benefit of all participants; the way that goods are traded, in order to benefit both producers and consumers; the way that economic activity is measured and counted, to ensure that priority is given to what is most worthwhile: in all of these areas a change of approach can greatly increase the total of human value from which everybody may benefit.

The adversarial character of democratic politics, however, tends much more towards the expectation of change than a cogent reality. For example: at the 2010 general election for the U.K. parliament, the Liberal Democrats wanted "every child to receive an excellent education, to unlock children's potential and to ensure that they can succeed in life"; Labour's goal was "educational excellence for every child, whatever their background or circumstances," and the Conservatives pledged to "improve standards for all pupils and close the attainment gap between the richest and poorest". The subtext is clear: "excellent education for *every* child"; "educational excellence for *every* child"; "improve standards for *all* pupils" – each seeking to address an educational system that closely mirrors and perpetuates the deep inequalities in British society. The desire for change is palpable, and each party has its own nostrums, but none articulates with any clarity what they think education is *for*. The reason for this is that each party is deeply and similarly conflicted on the question. But without a clear answer, an effective education policy is hard to pin down.

In the absence of such clarity, policy-making becomes an exercise in those untested nostrums – bright ideas inspired by the political discourse of change rather than specific human outcomes. For a picture of this, consider the number of Education Acts passed by the U.K. parliament in a fifty year period. There was one in each of 1962, 1964, 1967, 1968, 1973, 1975, 1976, 1979, 1980, 1981, 1986 (2), 1988, 1992, 1993, 1994, 1996, 1997, 2002, 2005, 2006, 2008 and 2011; twenty-three Education Acts, so described[1], and a further twenty-four acts with the word "education" in their title, as well as other acts touching upon education in the titles of which the word was not included[2]. In the same period there have been thirteen general elections and only six changes of governing party; so for each period of government by a political party an average of nearly four full Education Acts has been deemed necessary and an average of eight or more acts in total touching on education in a substantial way.

In health, there has been at least one significant piece of primary legislation bearing on the National Health Service every year since 1979, a period embracing only three changes of governing party. This reflects an increasing desire in government to micro-manage through legislation such a key area of social engagement, all the time protesting an intention to return power and autonomy to the people who supply and use NHS services. There is a conflict between an expressed political aspiration to "leave teaching to teachers and medicine to doctors" and a political reality in which the government takes the blame for failures and shortcomings wherever they occur. The unmet challenge, first to define a coherent set of social objectives and then to establish a framework in which they may be effectively delivered, has fallen foul of a narrow argument about public owner-

---

1   Including *Education and [something] Acts*, *Education (Schools) Acts* and *Education Reform Acts*.
2   *Academies* Acts, for example, and various *School* Acts.

ship and centralised direction versus competitive market forces, in
which the human relationships between the individual providers and
recipients of the service has been put to one side.

The framework that holds those relationships, the nature and quality of which have a profound effect upon the nature, quality and
effectiveness of the service that results, must provide healthy and
positive conditions in which they may flourish. Neither a govern-
ment-directed nor a market-driven model is likely to achieve this, for
in both cases the service provider is beholden to an interest group
other than the individual they are seeking to serve. Whether a doctor is contracted by the government or by a commercial provider
and its shareholders, the patient is a passive component in the terms
of that relationship, limited to whatever third party legal rights the
framework may happen to bestow. The doctor, therefore, may feel
bound to ask: "am I observing the terms of my contract?", rather
than "am I treating people in accordance with their individual wants
and needs?" It is hardly necessary to elaborate: anybody who has
worked in British education, healthcare or social services in the past
twenty years or more knows exactly what this means. It makes little
difference whether the service is provided commercially or directly
by government; both measure outcomes on a statistical cost-benefit
basis that places no express value on the human relationships upon
which the success of these social activities depends.

The focus on management, measurement and reorganisation,
which hangs over every aspect of government-funded service provision and is responsible for all those acts of parliament, stands as an
ineffectual substitute for intention and purpose in relation to services
that people are naturally motivated to provide for themselves. Mutuality – working together and helping one another out – is fundamental to the human state, and services such as the NHS, state-funded
education authorities and social care departments are simply organisational frameworks intended to support those fundamental human
impulses. The less these frameworks obtrude into the relationships
between the providers and the receivers of such services, and the less
mediated, or managed, the services are, the better the chance that

the human quality of the relationship will work its wonder, bringing benefits that may well be more profound for not being measurable in crude numerical terms.

For example, care workers responsible for elderly, infirm people still living in their homes, for whom they provide essential personal assistance, often work on a schedule where their visits may be 5, 15 or 30 minutes, and limited to the completion of a specific procedural task. They are paid only for the allotted duration of a visit, which means that they are not necessarily paid extra if the visit over-runs, nor for the time spent travelling from one visit to the next.[1] Under such conditions, their capacity to respond to the true human needs of the people they visit, to take the time to talk and listen, to carry out necessary additional tasks and build a caring relationship of trust and interdependence, is greatly curtailed. Worse than that, they are subtly (or not so subtly) encouraged by this organisational framework to treat their visits not as human encounters between equals but as process-driven, mechanistic tasks to which their clients are subject.

It is not difficult to unpick the sequence of incentives whereby this bizarre and inhuman arrangement has arisen. First, the responsible government provider, which is the local authority, has contracted out the service to a private, profit-making company, to whom they pay a negotiated price to discharge their obligations. The minimum extent of those obligations, which comprise both a service standard and a commitment to "value for money", is set down by central government, which provides much of the funding, so the local authority is effectively brokering between central government and a commercial provider a contractual arrangement that quantifies in extent and monetary value the care to be provided to the people in need.

Once that step is taken, the rest falls into place without further question. The provider company must perform the contracted services at minimum expense to its shareholders, in order to ensure their profit. With this in mind it naturally views its staff as a cost, to be kept to a minimum. Working out the minimum period of time in

1   Pennycook M., *Does it pay to care?* Resolution Foundation, 2013

which a "service" may be "delivered", and the lowest rate that may be paid, is the task of a manager for whom, within the terms of the contract, the true human needs of neither participant is a material consideration. The final step is to incentivise the staff to keep to their strict schedule. Paying them only for the allotted duration of a visit is a part of this, but not paying them for the period of travel between visits is the master stroke than ensures that they fit as many visits in as they possibly can. The fact that the rate of pay is low is of assistance with this, since only by doing as many visits as possible may these care workers earn the means for their own survival.

It is easy (and may be appropriate) to demonise the profit-making companies who vie for government contracts on such terms. It is important, however, to look to the top of the chain of causality, where sits a branch of government determined to award these contracts on a "value for money" basis, which means that they generally go to the cheapest supplier. A lower price necessarily entails lower wages and a reduction in the time spent on each visit; thus a model of efficiency designed to increase commercial profit is perversely applied in a social context in which both the low wages and the curtailed visits have negative consequences. If the principles of human value rather than commercial profit are applied, a visit to an elderly, housebound person, by a carer who can afford the time that they need, appears not as a cost to society but as a fundamental human benefit. The local authority, under pressure from central government, has got itself trapped in an economic framework that sets as its objective the task of reducing such visits to the minimum possible, when society would benefit far more if as much time as possible was spend by people engaging with and caring for one another at every level.

IF THE TASK of politics is to create space and opportunity for people to assert their natural propensity to get on with and look after one another, how would it achieve this? The answer is clearly not another institutional reorganisation, such as those that have beset the NHS over much of its lifetime. But what about *de*-organisation – the dismantling of the organisational frameworks that prevent people from engaging one with another? Technology has shown the way: the internet has connected producers directly to consumers by providing an electronic showcase for their work and an electronic means of ordering and paying for it. But politically the tendency has been in quite the other direction. The determination of successive governments in Britain and elsewhere to introduce competition into relationships that were once straightforward has led, as we have seen, to complex monopolies often more pernicious than the state monopolies they replaced, and ruled over by swollen regulatory bureaucracies.

It is true that some state monopolies were once a by-word for inefficiency and poor service, but largely because they were starved of capital and were subject to the whims and abuses of a shifting party politics unable to decide whether it wanted subsidised public services or profitable enterprises – either a call upon or a contributor to the public purse. Privatisation was intended to settle the argument, but failed to do so because utilities such as electricity, gas, water, postal deliveries, telecommunications, roads, railways and bus services (among others) remain public services in the public mind, with the government ultimately liable for the quality and price of the provision.

To explore this further, consider how the insurance market works. This is an industry that has never, in the popular mind, been publicly owned. In fact, however, vast tracts of it are state administered in Britain, for how else should we describe a free national health service and a universal state pension, especially one part-funded by a tax called National Insurance? Furthermore, the origins of both general and life insurance lie in mutual societies, the profits of which were returned to their policy holder members, and it is only because the industry is now so huge, so commercialised and so heavily marketed that it is so easily forgotten how much nearer to a social service than a consumer product it really is. It reflects a natural aspect of human socialisation, in which people look after one another in the expectation of benefiting from the support of the community in their own time of need. Such mutuality could scarcely be more central to the human experience. People who co-operate are more likely to flourish, which is why evolution has selected for our ability to get on with one another in this way.

At first sight, the insurance industry appears to supply a human need for economic security and reassurance, and in so far as it does this it may be said to offer human value. Look more deeply, however, and it soon becomes apparent that the industry only circulates wealth rather than creates it: the human value lies not in those circulating transactions but in the willingness of people to pool their risks in support of each other. It follows that insurance companies do not supply insurance as such, but merely commercialise and profit from a human propensity to insure one another. The money they pay out in claims originates with and, arguably, belongs to all the people who participate in sharing their risks.

The industry supplies a framework within which people may insure each other. This framework may be useful but it does not have human value as such. It is a cost upon the human willingness to pool risk and, as such, something of which society wants as little as is strictly necessary. If, every time a house burned down, the owner's bank account were to be credited with the amount of the loss, and everybody else's account deducted a penny or two to pay for it, the job would be done with the minimum possible transactional intervention – just a straight call upon the community to replace the lost wealth out of the collective surplus[1]. This is why large organisations and governments often "self-insure". Their size is such that they can pool their own risks, riding the ups and downs knowing that they are statistically likely, over time, to suffer average losses. Since their premiums would have to cover both those losses and an insurance company's overheads, it is better value not to buy insurance at all.

A government working in the interests of its people might seek to assist them to self-insure in this way, pooling individual risks and covering each other's losses at minimum cost, where cost is not the premiums required to pay legitimate claims but the whole paraphernalia and transactional activity of the insurance industry, including the huge sums spent on advertising, sales staff, commissions to

---

1   The annual cost per household of this arrangement would have been about £16 in 2012.

brokers, promotions, websites, unsolicited telephone calls, etc., etc., all of which are added to the customers premiums. Research on UK motor insurance[1], for example, shows that in 2011 26% of premium income was spent on general overheads, which includes advertising and sales expenses; 3% covered uninsured drivers; 20% was spent on whiplash and a further 15% on other personal injury claims (excluding "catastrophic claims"). Of those latter figures, about a third went on legal costs; as a minimum, therefore, we can say that 40% of the money paid for motor insurance was not returned to the people who paid the insurance premiums. Consider, in addition, that whiplash claims are increasing, while the number of recorded accidents is falling, and it is clear that many such claims are either fraudulent or "automatic" – smallish sums pursued by claims management companies without reference to specific injuries sustained by their clients. Add this to the total and it is possible that as little as half of what is paid in premiums is returned legitimately to the people insured.

Here is the transactional economy in action: the cost of acquiring business and attempting to make a profit; the legal costs of arguing about claims and seeking to maximise them; the casual (and deliberate) frauds and delinquencies, considered "victimless" because they are believed to be perpetrated against profit-making corporations who are themselves out for all they can get. To address these issues, and to help people to insure with as little cost as possible, a government must first unpick the conundrum that has seen the human impulse for mutual support descend into a hugely profitable industry that employs 320,000 people and which owns much of the prime real estate in the City of London. How might it "de-organise" such a complex and wasteful system, to bring the benefits of insurance much more directly to the people who both pay for and make use of it? At the heart of that question sits the tangled concept of "fairness", a seemingly unimpeachable quality upon which rests, nonetheless, at least part of the responsibility for every bureaucratic descent into waste and complexity.

---

1   *Lifting the bonnet on car insurance - what are the real costs?* Association of British Insurers report, March 2013

FAIRNESS USED TO describe the human quality of treating people well out of goodness and generosity, rather than entitlement. Politics has degraded that high-mindedness, however, and now it has become a "dog-whistle" to voters by politicians promising to correct some perceived wrong, particularly in relation to people's sense of entitlement. A perception of unfairness is easy to generate, and is just as easily turned towards feelings of prejudice and ill-will.

People are vulnerable to exploitation when they deny themselves the free benefits of collaboration for fear of being "taken advantage of" by collaborators who may not "pull their weight". Fairness may be harmful, therefore, when it denies people a collective and equal good on the grounds of differential entitlement. In the case of motor insurance, it would be a great advantage collectively if premiums were set at a flat rate – the same for everyone. They would drop significantly, on average, but many people with the lowest premiums would pay more to make up for the higher-risk drivers. Such an arrangement appears, on the face of it, sufficiently unfair to be a political non-starter; and yet, collectively, the saving on overheads, advertising, marketing, administration and risk assessment – would be a billion or two pounds a year in lower premiums, which is probably enough to give every primary age child in the land a free hot meal at lunchtime.

The benefits of a regular, nutritious lunch has been amply demonstrated in developmental terms, which is why, in 2014, they are being introduced for the youngest schoolchildren. As a social investment it is likely to pay a handsome return, with lower demand for health, social care and even criminal justice services in the future, which will benefit everybody. The connection between lower motor premiums and free school lunches is, however, tenuous at best, and turning the one into the other is not something that a government can achieve by a stroke of a pen, or even an act of parliament. It requires that people embrace the benefit that flows from a collective gain, even if it is not to their short term or immediate advantage.

The established precedents are clear to see. People contribute to hospitals and schools, irrespective of whether or how much they personally use them; and that they do so on the basis of what they are deemed able to afford rather than their usage is an illustration of how flexible the term "fair" has become in the political lexicon. In the case of established public services, it is considered "fair" that the better off should contribute more and "unfair" when they fail to do so. Viewed in this light, a flat rate for car insurance could as plausibly appear unfair for taking no account of people's varying means, as it does for not reflecting the higher risk of certain drivers.

The parallels go deeper: car insurance is a general, public benefit, because anybody can be caught up in an accident that is not their fault. For this reason it is mandatory: it acknowledges an interdependence of people's lives and actions that makes it as much a social as a personal service. As a social service, the argument that a person's contribution should be correlated to their risk factors sits oddly in a society where healthcare and education are freely and equally provided to smokers, alcoholics, sky-divers, dyslexics, delinquents and any other group that is disproportionately expensive to treat or educate. The pattern, however, varies greatly around the world. Some countries expect everybody to buy private health insurance, in which case smokers and sky-divers may well pay more; some offer free child-care; some offer free school meals. The distinction between services that are provided freely and equally and those that are paid for is not rooted in any notion of "fairness" as an absolute human value but depends on the history, custom and expectation in different states.

Flat rate car insurance is probably a good idea, all in all, and the fact that it may be deemed unfair for two opposing reasons can only augment its credibility. Here, however, it stands merely as a counter-intuitive provocation, illustrative of how the eradication of an entire marketplace can produce a service that is much less wasteful of human effort. It is counter-intuitive because, since the 1980s, the direction of policy, embracing governments nominally of both right and left, has been in the opposite direction, creating competitive structures in areas of activity such as public utilities where none, previously, existed – not even in the Victorian times so often cited as the model and inspiration for the social and economic experiments of the Thatcher years.

As a consequence of those experiments the principle of fairness has been thoroughly interwoven with the related concept of "deserving". This is the fairness of the free, competitive market, in which insurance companies, their actuaries and underwriters work hard to give everybody a policy quotation that matches their particular circumstances most closely – the quote that they "deserve". With this approach, market prices are fair by definition, because if lower or higher prices were achievable the market mechanism would supply them. Everybody gets what they deserve, including the newly privatised utility companies, whose profits are justified by the commercial risks to which the state-backed providers were not exposed.

As we saw in Chapter 2, however, whenever these newly competitive markets for basic commodity services such as energy, water, telecommunications, postal services, the railways, etc. have been instituted, governments have been forced to create regulatory bureaucracies to ensure that they operate "fairly", counteracting the tendency towards the market monopolies and cartels that invariably emerge in a "captive market", when the product is an essential one that people have no option but to purchase. Similarly, the financial services industry, which, as its name suggests, also has a primary public service function, has numerous tiers of regulation, all struggling to ensure that people do not get ripped off in a competitive market in which "service" turns out to be nothing more elevated than a route to colossal profits. Creating markets because they are fair, watching them operate unfairly and then creating regulators to distort them back towards a semblance of fairness is, quite obviously, both wasteful and expensive, and illustrates how the high-minded concept of fairness is so easily degraded into a system of opaque and arbitrary rules, adding layers of organisational complexity and manifold possibilities for exploitation. It begs the question, if government wants the banks, utilities, and other providers to act in the best interests of society, why not set them up as public interest companies in the first place? And once it has done so, why not invite them to collaborate with one another, sharing best practice, streamlining their operations by stripping out the cost of competing for profit?

When it comes to the way that wealth is distributed, the concept of "deserving" is conflated with "earning", on the market-driven principle that whatever people earn is the accurate measure of what they deserve for the work they contribute. The parents of young children, when in receipt of state benefits, are actively encouraged into paid work at the earliest opportunity, at which point government is quite happy to pick up the tab for their childcare costs, even when this may be as much as the benefits they were previously receiving or as much again as they are earning. For only in paid work can their degree of "deserving" be assessed, an approach the validity of which is called seriously into question when one considers the extent to which governments are obliged to augment the incomes of people whose "fair" and "deserved" earnings do not allow them sufficient to live on. In Britain, although much is heard about the work-shy and "undeserving", much more Housing Benefit, tax credit and other financial support is paid to people in work than to the unemployed. If the work of employees can be valued so little, it raises a question about the true value and usefulness of paid employment, and whether it is something that a government should necessarily seek to encourage.

To give this some context: the 320,000 people employed in the UK insurance industry is similar to the number of nurses employed in the entire NHS; it is not much fewer than the total employed in agricultural production, growing Britain's food; and it is more than twice the number employed in the water, gas and electricity industries combined, according to insurance industry figures. That latter figure is quite telling: it takes twice as many people to circulate wealth through the insurance market as it does to create the wealth of essential products such as water and energy delivered to the home. In fact, much more than that, for those utility companies themselves engage in much wasted transactional activity, as everybody knows who has ever been subject to a high-pressure sales pitch. And speaking of sales pitches, the number of estate and property agents in Britain rose in 2013 to well over 500,000, none of whom is generating any new wealth, but are merely extracting a transactional margin from every sale that they broker.

Transactional activity is a cost upon society, not a wealth producer. The wealth that goes to pay transactional workers is not, therefore, lost to society if their employment ceases, but is gained back, and available to be redirected towards something more useful. In that sense, unnecessary insurance overheads really can be turned into hot meals for school children; it only requires that those insurance sales-people and clerks (whom society has shown it can afford to pay) redirect their labour towards the growing, cooking and serving of food in the nation's schools. If that sounds like a throwback to the Cultural Revolution, when intellectuals and teachers were marched out into the paddy fields of China, it must be emphasised that it is not something that a government can direct. After all, the money originates with the "paying public", who must be willing to divert it towards this end.

On this question of spending, the British, in particular, are highly conflicted, their politics labouring under the burden of legacy constraints arising from the two competing political impulses of the 20th century. Socialism dictates that there are certain things that a state must do; capitalism dictates that people behave out of economic self-interest and should fend for themselves. The first is represented by the collectivist spirit of the National Health Service and public education, which people are generally happy to fund through their taxes; the second by a strong cultural bias in favour of independent home ownership, underpinned by the capitalist nirvana of ever-rising house prices. Both have become institutionalised in the British political psyche, and politicians tinker with them at their peril.

This tension, bordering on conflict, between the politics of mutual support and individual self-interest is no longer played out openly between the parties. Instead, all sides in such debates are locked into the old-established assumptions, which is why the term "legacy constraints" is appropriate. The right-leaning Conservative party's 2010 manifesto stated: "As the party of the NHS, we will never change the idea at its heart – that healthcare in this country is free at the point of use and available to everyone based on need, not ability to pay," while the left-leaning Labour party endorsed home ownership as a route to wealth, observing that "people want to know that their living standards and quality of life will improve. So we will enable more people to get on the housing ladder." The fact that rising house prices suck wealth out of the real economy, which is then not available in the form of mutual human services such as the NHS and state education, scarcely features in the political discourse.

From this starting point, many equally entrenched assumptions follow. From both ends of the political spectrum, that vexed notion of "fairness" is invoked to suggest that only paid employment entitles a person to earn what they "deserve" to live. In 2010, Labour pledged that "all those who can work will be required to do so," while the Conservatives insisted that "unemployed people must be prepared to take up job offers" and threatened to penalise them if they did not do so. The availability of paid employment is sometimes called into question in the political debate, but its quality and usefulness almost never are, just as the implications of J M Keynes' letter to his grandchildren are completely forgotten. Keynes anticipated that increases in productivity made possible by technological advances would reduce paid employment to as little as 15 hours per week by the early 21st century, and it is highly likely that he underestimated those advances and the increases in productivity to which they could lead. In Britain, however, in the years leading up to 2014, productivity has been falling; the investment that would increase it has been replaced by increasingly insecure employment at levels of pay that are falling in real terms. It may be cheaper for investors, and necessary for their employees, that people should work more and more, for low wages, to sustain their living. Thus, however, are they deprived of one of the key ingredients for the creation of human value, to which Keynes looked forward, which is self-directed time.

"It will remain reasonable to be economically purposive for others after it has ceased to be reasonable for oneself," Keynes wrote[1],

---

1   Keynes J.M., *Economic Possibilities for our Grandchildren*, (1930)

anticipating a time when the willingness of people to exert themselves beyond the production of their own economic needs would arise from a desire to contribute most effectively to the general wellbeing. With the hindsight of over eighty years, that must seem optimistic, but it reflects a present reality in that the current focus on paid employment is inefficient at deploying human resources to the general good. Neither of the opposing systems that defined the political fault-lines of the 20th century has proved effective in this respect. The imposed collectivity of socialism could not accommodate the principle of self-directed time in the economic sphere; in the competitive world of market capitalism, significant self-directed time is a luxury restricted to the fortunate few.

The true needs of elderly people requiring care and company in their homes are much better met by people working in their own time, than when forced to count every paid minute. And how much less wasteful of human time and effort would it be for people to look after their own children, if they would like to, or paint their own houses, than to travel to work to earn the money to pay others to travel to their houses to do these tasks for them? Added to this is the social advantage of people working out of their own will and moral purpose: for no amount of money can engage a care worker to be kind, warm and attentive to the more subtle, unstated needs of the people whom they visit, unless they are willing. Generally they are more than willing, overflowing with both capacity and motivation, and lack only the opportunity and the time to engage in this way.

WE HAVE ARRIVED at a picture of a society so productive that it wants for little in a material way; that applies its wealth to its present needs, storing only the minimum bespoken by prudence; that applies its extensive self-directed time to its own self-improvement and a profound, mutually beneficial engagement with others. We want only the means of bringing it about, and we acknowledge that it is not to be achieved by executive fiat or political debate, but through the free and self-willed participation of the society's members. The question for politics, therefore, is how can the conditions be created that will allow such a society to evolve out of its own determination?

Those legacy constraints, of which we spoke, pulling left, pulling right, pulling against each other until they can pull no more and just seize up somewhere near an indefinable middle: they operate upon the body politic like strained muscles in a real body, preventing free movement and in need of therapy to de-contract them and allow them to heal. In their tense, contracted state they cause that body to fight over resources that it feels to be limited – under resourced NHS; low wages and insecure employment; a sense of economic precariousness and fear of losing out – in the face of which rising house prices offer the palliative care of a drug with habit-forming tendencies. This provides the temporary relief of making people feel richer, so they can borrow more; but the repayments on those borrowings must come from insecure income, both increasing the pressure to find paid work and reducing the wealth available for immediate needs.

The key to successful change is to provide an alternative that is manifestly better, and in this respect the "bright idea" approach of serial reorganisation – the approach that brought all those Education Acts and health service reforms – has a poor track record. It is not the chop and change of policy that comes with different governments and different ministers that is needed, but real alternatives, allowing people much greater freedom in the choice of their path. Nor are we speaking, here, of the "choice agenda" that has atomised public services to create an illusion of variety: the choice required is not the reactive response of a passive consumer, but the active choice of the provider and doer, in the way that they go about the business of engaging with their fellow humans.

The specific proposals of previous chapters – for new forms of corporate governance; for new parameters to trade; for a new model of land ownership; for a new way of measuring human output – all provide new outlets for human energy and activity on terms of equal advantage to the established forms, thus helping to rediscover the movement and flexibility that will guide the body politic out of its existing paralysis. The central proposal of Chapter 10, concerning limited liability, illustrates how this works. State-sponsored, legal protection for shareholders is difficult to justify for companies the

only purpose of which is shareholder profit, if only because it gives
other, more socially benevolent forms of enterprise very little chance
to compete for capital. If investors were to weigh up the relative risk
of a fixed interest return combined with limited liability, versus the
opportunity for capital gain combined with unlimited liability for
all a company's debts, the attractiveness of social investment could
increase enormously. The word *could* is important in that sentence.
Instead of prescribing how business should be done, the purpose of
human politics is to shake up the whole system of work, risk and
reward, to de-institutionalise established norms, give oxygen to innovative forms and allow human energy and aspiration to embrace a
more dynamic set of choices.

This approach sits in the spirit of the "nudge theory" discussed in
Chapter 8. Although conceived as a way of steering individual people
towards actions more likely to be good for them, the idea of nudging organisational and bureaucratic behaviour has potentially more
far-reaching consequences. It holds out the prospect of changing not
just individual instances of behaviour, but the underlying expectations, which in turn promotes more profoundly shifting patterns of
behaviour. In relation to land ownership, the political and economic
imperatives in Britain are sharply divergent, since rising house prices, while politically attractive, tie up useful wealth and suck both
investment and consumption out of the economy. To resolve this
divergence, the deep-seated policy assumptions of planners, landowners, developers, mortgage brokers and lenders, as well as those
who direct the tax and fiscal policy of central government, need to
be loosened up and exposed to new models of land ownership and
alternative ways of doing business.

This approach, of creating opportunities for new, socially progressive models of economic activity to compete at least on equal terms
with the existing, has a better chance of improving outcomes than
the top-down directives to which politicians generally resort in pursuit of their ambitious programmes of reform. In the case of trade,
the approach of nation states has been invariably self-interested, up
to the point where it is quite normal to talk about "the international

race to succeed in the global market place" – a competition that has become a race to the bottom for workers in many countries struggling to retain for themselves a reasonable share of their productive capacity. That race is won or lost on the basis of an aggregation of a nation's wealth; it does not reference the individual circumstances of a nation's people and takes no notice whatsoever of the individual circumstances of the people in the nation with which the trade is being conducted. As such, it is fundamentally useless as a measure of individual or even social wellbeing when expressed in terms of human value.

WHEN PEOPLE ARE required to pay twice as much (or more) for their houses than the value of the work of construction that they contain, and when so much of the price of the products they buy is siphoned off in transactional activity and shareholder profit, they find themselves obliged to labour much longer, struggling to amass far more wealth than they realistically need, merely to compensate for all that is lost to them by being stored away in land values, company shares and bank accounts around the world, many of them inaccessible to the tax authorities of the countries from which the money was derived. If this colossal waste of work could be avoided, people labouring less to sustain their quality of life would have more of the self-directed time so essential for healthy self-development, be less inclined to begrudge others and, therefore, more inclined to embrace the social risks of collaborating. Uninhibited collaboration tends rapidly to increased useful productivity, from which a virtuous cycle of increasing real wealth and ever more productive human relationships can be set in motion.

The elevation of alternative, socially benevolent, models of activity to a position of competitive equality with the free market is the first stage towards re-balancing the economy away from transactional gain and in favour of producing the true human value upon which this cycle depends. Many such models exist already, developed by social entrepreneurs and third sector organisations, and on a small scale by thousands of community and self-help groups. Many others have been developed in concept, but the scope for realisation is limited in a sector still ploughing its lonely furrows in the stony margins of great, lush fields awash with capital in pursuit of the highest possible financial return. The outcome, in human social terms, then depends upon whether those socially benevolent models are able to prosper in an equal environment. The challenge remains one of more equal distribution: distribution of wealth, certainly, but more importantly the distribution of the means of producing it, including both capital resources such as land and equipment, and the self-directed time that is so essential if people are to add value in their own lives.

An economic framework that is focused less upon accumulating and storing wealth, and more upon applying it in the form of human value, is likely of itself to increase access and reduce disparity. Ultimately, however, it can provide only a context, which contains the opportunity for people to apply the principles of mutuality and inclusiveness if they choose. No system of law or custom can maintain this context and keep alive the opportunity if people are determined to reassert their narrow self-interest. That is why, alongside the promotion of new forms of doing business, government has a whole other task of promoting the advancement of the human will, from which mutual understanding and shared interest naturally arise. The way in which it seeks to regulate human behaviour on behalf of society, and the way it seeks to educate children growing up in that society, are central to its success in this vital realm, and are the subjects of the concluding chapters.

Chapter 13

BREAKING THE MOULD

Achieving change in a climate of conformity

"WHEREAS THE DRINKING of spirituous liquors and strong waters is become very common, especially among the people of lower and inferior ranks, the constant and excessive use whereof tends greatly to the destruction of their health, renders them unfit for useful labor and business, debauching their morals, and inciting them to perpetrate all manner of vices..."

So reads the preamble to the Gin Act of 1736, one of many legislative attempts to curb the excesses of the "gin craze" that took hold in England in the early 18th century. Gin arrived from Holland with William of Orange, received political encouragement as a rival to French brandy and offered profits to landowners by creating a market for grain that was not otherwise fit for human consumption. But as consumption increased it also created social mayhem; the government felt compelled to legislate but did so inconsistently, with several attempts required to bring the situation under control.

The problem, according to one source, was price, with "gin and other spirituous liquors ... being sold at a very low rate [to] the meaner though useful part of the nation, such as day-laborers, men and women servants, and common soldiers...[1]" The solutions adopted were licensing and duty, with increasingly severe punishments for unlicensed supply. The government hoped by these means to make gin less affordable and less accessible, and therefore less likely to

---

1   Jackson R., *Considerations on the Increase of Crime*, London 1828

keep this "meaner though useful part of the nation" from its allotted domestic drudgery or punishing physical work.

Three centuries later, neither the problem nor the proposed solutions have materially changed. Problem-drinking is rife, both in public and, more harmfully, in private, where it sits at the root of an epidemic of domestic violence. To combat it, the successors of those licensing laws remain in force, along with the duty on alcohol for which minimum pricing is now proposed, and the diversity of the interests that collide over the issue has also changed little since the 18th century. The manufacturers and the distributors are protective of their profitable markets, just as those landowners were pleased to have an outlet for their sub-standard grain. The social consequences, however, of alcohol, in health and public order terms, remain unacceptable.

Government has a social role to play in directing people's wants, provided it can take them with it. Tobacco manufacturers report that cigarette consumption fell in Britain by 50% between 1990 and 2012, as fewer people smoke, and do so less often. Among other measures, successive governments have raised duty to increased prices, restricted advertising and sponsorship, required health warnings on packets and banned smoking in places where people gather. These steps are effective both because they are enforceable and because they underpin people's own sense of responsibility, now that the dangers of passive smoking are widely accepted. It is true that outright prohibition, which relates to younger smokers, is ineffective. 10% of 15 year-olds were, in 2012, classified as regular smokers, as were 15% of the 16 to 19 age group. These figures compare with 20% of the population as a whole, and suggests that if young people wish to by tobacco products they will usually find a way. Even so, the incidence of smoking has fallen more rapidly among young people than it has among people of working age.

Is this, therefore, a Goldilocks scenario, where the policy is just right: as effective as it can be without being actively harmful? Not entirely: contraband and counterfeit cigarettes have become much more common as prices have risen, so tax income is lost and health risks heightened, since counterfeit cigarettes are of uncontrolled provenance and content. Even more corrosive are the social effects of organised crime, which controls much of the illegal trade. The higher the tax on tobacco, the greater the scope for illegal profit, much of which is channelled into other avenues of crime.

Controls, nudges and prohibitions can only achieve so much, before they start to do harm. Some towns have persuaded shops to remove high-strength, cheap beers and ciders from their shelves. The problem appears solved when the homeless people who drink them move on to a place where they are still available. But it is no more solved than alcohol-fuelled violence is solved when it moves from the street to the home in the form of domestic abuse. Homelessness, alcoholism and domestic violence all embrace a range of economic, educational, emotional and mental health problems that will only be solved when acknowledged for what they are.

Smoking correlates with wealth and social status, with people in the poorest category nearly four times more likely to smoke than those in the wealthiest. The duty levied on tobacco falls, therefore, disproportionately on the people least able to pay it, a regressive tax of over £6 per packet which compounds the poverty-related ills that cause people to smoke in the first place. "Poverty-related smoking" is a broad characterisation of a habit intended to relieve stress in conditions where other avenues of escape are unavailable; combine this with educational deficit, low aspiration and a poor understanding of health issues, and a stark picture emerges of smoking connected to a cycle of deprivation, which, in many cases, proves heritable.

A government that wishes to reduce the worst effects of drinking or smoking must address not the bottle or the cigarette packet but the circumstances of marginalisation and deprivation in which the problems related to them are most persistent. Coercive or controlling measures will not stop people doing things that, for whatever reason, they have chosen. However promising these measures appear, they end up at the bottom of a blind alley: in the face of failed coercion more punitive sanctions are applied, which show a rapidly diminishing return on the cost of imposing them.

Nowhere is this truth more brutally exposed than in the "war on drugs" that has wrought such global havoc in the past 40 years. In Britain, as elsewhere, the consumption of heroin, cocaine, cannabis and their multiple derivatives and synthetic competitors is driven by a simple truth – that people want to consume them. The reasons may be good or bad, harmless or harmful, but they do not deny the want. For decades, drugs prevention efforts have been focused on prohibition; punishments are harsh, prisons overflowing. Governments never go so wrong, however, as when they forget how dependent they are upon the consent of the governed. A society that wishes to reduce drug consumption and its associated harms must address the reasons for that want, rather than attempt to frustrate it.

The use of illegal drugs has fallen in recent years, but there were still 2.7 million users (aged 16 to 59) in England and Wales in 2012-13, compared to about 7.5 million smokers. Nearly 12 million people (well over a third of those surveyed) report having taken an illegal drug at some point in their lives. Prohibition is more likely to distort or displace the problem than to solve it. Speed cameras slow people down, so long as they spot them, but they do not stop them wanting to drive at a speed dictated by their own judgement, which is what they do before and after the speed camera is passed. Similarly, as drugs prohibition rages, enterprising dealers duck and dive to confound the rules, cooking up a dizzying list of synthetic alternatives of dubious legality and composition. The effect of prohibition has been to throw away the management rulebook: since drugs may not be cultivated, processed, bought, sold, shared, given away, or even possessed, there is nothing to manage and the framework for production and distribution is entirely in the hands of criminal cartels.

Drug users must fend for themselves in an unregulated and often dangerous market, in which they demonstrate a remarkable capacity for self-management. That only a quarter of the people who have ever taken illegal drugs still do so belies the hackneyed image of all drug users as helpless addicts or junkies. The majority are in control of their use, which extends also to the basics of saying alive. NHS figures suggest that about 87,000 deaths per year in England and

Wales of those aged 35 and over are caused by smoking – over 1% of current smokers. In comparison, the best guess for deaths caused by taking illegal drugs is about 1,500 per year, or 0.05% of current users – one twentieth of the rate. Since, however, many of the most serious health risks of illegal drug use arise from the uncontrolled nature of the supply, this low death toll cannot be chalked up as a success for prohibition policy. It is often the substances used to bulk up illegally traded drugs that present the greatest risk of physical harm, together with the associated risk of overdose from not knowing how much of a drug a dose actually contains.

These and other drugs-related harms are greater than they would be if the drugs were not illegal. Regulate content, strength, purity and price, encourage the use of clean needles, and the harms that remain – to the user, and those connected to them – become much easier to manage, well away from the revolving door of the criminal justice system and its fruitless expenditure of resources. As with alcohol and tobacco, many of the most problematic drug users acquire their habit as a form of pain relief from the anguish of emotionally trying lives. Criminalisation compounds that harm without doing anything to relieve the pain or address the incapacity to deal with it. Prisons are full of drugs-related offenders whose lives are permanently blighted at huge public expense. For young people, even if they avoid incarceration, a drugs-related criminal record is often more harmful to their life prospects than the drugs they have used.

When government surrenders control of the drugs trade to the criminal cartels, it limits its own capacity to manage the associated harms. At a global level, governments and international institutions committed the the war on drugs have surrendered as much as 1% of the global economy, running to hundreds of billions of U.S. dollars, into criminal hands. The huge profits this generates fund arms trading, people trafficking and exploitation on an industrial scale, while fuelling conflicts in producer countries in which thousands of people are killed every year. On streets across the world, gangs fight for control of distribution networks, while the prices they charge feed into further lawbreaking when users take to petty crime to fund their purchases. That the war on drugs has failed comprehensively to improve human wellbeing is widely accepted: politicians, policy-makers, civil servants, judges, lawyers, police officers, prison officers, health professionals, social workers, academics, investigative journalists – almost everybody who has researched the subject or encountered it in their professional lives – knows full well that the harms caused by the global war on drugs are entirely disproportionate to any benefits that it brings.

THE WAR ON DRUGS makes no sense, but merely to say so will achieve little. Clearly it makes sense to some people, some of the time, or it wouldn't be happening. It makes sense to the person in the Home Office, whose job it is, every time someone calls for a relaxation of British drugs laws, to rush out a statement saying there will be no change. It makes sense in the same way that it makes sense to suppose that economic growth is best achieved through a system that drags wealth inexorably upwards towards those who already have far more than they need, leaving mounting poverty, including middle class poverty, in its wake. It makes sense because it has to make sense: the people who might change the direction of policy are stuck in a place that makes such change impossible to imagine.

At the heart of the problem lies a structural adherence to the status quo, with which all established government is encumbered. The word "govern" means "to steer" and the nature of established power is to keep things "steady as they are". Traditionally, state religion plays a central role in maintaining the established order; by locating the rewards of conformity beyond the grave, it encourages people to put up with hardships that they otherwise might resist more actively. In secular democracies it is often said that shopping is the new religion, but this is not entirely accurate. Much more like a religion is what makes shopping possible, which is easy consumer credit. Consumer credit is religion on steroids: rooted in a blind faith that the future will provide for the repayments, it grants rewards to be consumed immediately rather than depending upon the intangibles of an uncertain afterlife. All it asks is that faith should endure: that

people will continue to believe in the capacity of their future prospects to sustain their indebtedness.

Indebtedness is key to the established order. Today's wage-slaves
may be more comfortable in material terms, but, with their 95%
mortgages and their groaning credit cards, they are no less chained,
for practical purposes, to their task and station than were the mediaeval peasantry, who lived in fear both of their overlords and the
last judgement. Britain's national obsession with house prices reflects
this. As prices rise, the debt diminishes as a proportion, but even a
small fall may send the value of a house below the amount that has
been borrowed to buy it. Add in the rising burden of student debt,
tens of thousands of pounds of which graduates take into their working lives, together with credit card debt, bank overdrafts, car loans,
holiday loans, home improvement loans, personal loans, and short-
term, pay-day loans at exorbitant rates of interest, and it is clear that
for many people "judgement day" comes round all too soon and all to
frequently. In an echo of the way that peasants were once "owned"
by those feudal overlords, many people today are now owned by
their lenders, not all of whom play nicely when it comes to the business of recovering their loans.

Indebtedness undermines a key component of human wellbeing, which is autonomy, and replaces it with fear of instability and
a consequent reluctance to change. Mortgage debt may contribute,
through house price rises, to the accumulation of a substantial asset,
but it has no cash value until people sell the roof that shelters them.
Britain's households divide into three socio-economic groups, the
first of which is asset rich, either mortgage free or nearly so; the second is mortgage-encumbered; the third is renting, at a cost as much
or even greater than the repayments on a mortgage but with little
prospect of accumulating an alternative equivalent asset. Of these,
only the last – and least powerful – has an interest in challenging the
firm grip of indebtedness upon society. Everybody else has locked
themselves into the debt paradigm, with a strong interest in keeping
the credit flowing into rising house prices.

This is how governments like it. Abundant credit is a quick route to GDP growth and immediate economic contentment. Long-term indebtedness makes political and social stability a much easier electoral sell, which gives incumbent governments an advantage and causes their main rivals to pledge continuity of economic management in their pitch to the voters. This preference for stability and continuity over deep change strays almost naturally from the economic to the social context. When it comes to drugs, most voters have limited personal experience, so the facts that they are (a) illegal and (b) known to be harmful are sufficient to create a strong antipathy towards reform. The further fact that much of the harm arises *because* the drugs are illegal has little impact because those effects, too, are largely hidden. Information reaches people via news reports of distant, drugs-related conflicts, or television and film dramas set in gritty, fictionalised contexts that shy away from the objective mundane in favour of tension and jeopardy. These associations with the illegal drugs trade create a feedback loop that reinforces negative perceptions of drugs and underpins prohibition, even though their worst effects arise from prohibition rather than the drugs themselves.

Across politics, the same principle applies: deep change can always be made to look dangerous. The endless cycle of reform and reorganisation described in Chapter 12 – all those policy "bright ideas" that find their way into successive Education Acts, Health Acts, and so forth – are aimed not at changing the system but at more deeply entrenching it, by adding new layers of management and control. The standard political response to something that is failing to work is *reactive*, to manage it more tightly and try to force it to do what it should. This approach plays well in the short term, since people like to believe that their government is in control. But it means that the deeper questions about why the system is broken are never asked.

British politics is beset with reactionary trigger-issues of this sort, in which politicians seek to "disappear" problems rather than to solve them. Crime and immigration are the headline examples, spoken of almost in the same breath as if the one is as bad as the other. Both involve locking people up, which is one way of removing the problem from the public gaze; the U.K. has one of the largest immigration detention operations in Europe, while the prison population in England and Wales has more or less doubled in the last 20 years. The trick is to re-frame the issue in a more favourable light. Crime is a social problem, difficult for politicians to control, but re-frame it in terms of punishment – that punishments are too lenient – and possible courses of action immediately arise. In 1993, 16% of people sentenced for indictable offences went to prison; ten years later this had risen to 28%, while the sentences they received continued to get longer and the number of people in prison continued to rise[1].

Sentencing is highly visible, but prison itself is not. If tougher sentencing solves the political problem, nobody is much interested in where all those prisoners are to go. At the end of 2013 the Prison Service reported that there were 120 prisons in England and Wales, housing 83,640 prisoners at an average of 697 per prison. The average *un-crowded* capacity was 633, which means that an additional twelve, average-sized prisons were needed immediately to eliminate the over-crowding, while many of the existing ones were run-down and in need of replacement or repair. A new prison would also be required for every 0.75% further rise in prisoner numbers. Building new prisons is hugely expensive and takes years in the planning, and each prisoner costs tens of thousands of pounds a year to house. Locking people up may "disappear" them from daily life, but the desire to appear tough on crime soon comes up against the realities of the public finances.

Just before the crash of 2008 the prison population was already 83,000, and rising fast towards the 100,000 level. The government projected in 2006 that with no change in sentencing policy there would be 90,000 prisoners by 2010 and 98,000 by 2013, so it finally bit the bullet and announced plans to spend £3.8bn to create 20,000 new places. But the new super-prisons never happened; the prison population peaked at 87,000 in late 2011 and by the end of 2013 it was back to the level of six years previously. A political problem

1 *Story of the Prison Population: 1993 – 2012 England and Wales*, Ministry of Justice, January 2013

solved in a reactive way by increasing sentences had created a new, practical problem requiring a pro-active solution, and without new prisons an alternative approach had to be found. Fortunately for the government, people coming out of prison are scarcely more visible than those inside. Since no one was really looking, below-the-radar pragmatism could be brought to bear.

Prison doesn't work as a punishment: the statistical correlation between the amount of crime and the number of people in prison is weak and there is plenty of evidence that community sentencing, allied with well-resourced probation services, is much more effective in reducing re-offending and helping the public to feel safe. Building more prisons, therefore, never made policy sense; instead, the high profile increases in the severity of sentencing through the 1990s and 2000s were quietly offset in the latter part of that period by a sharp increase in early release, including the widespread adoption of the Home Detention Curfew scheme, better known as electronic tagging. The government got people out of prison faster in order to let more in, giving a new meaning to the term "revolving door" and tacitly acknowledging that many offenders did not need to be in prison for the purpose of public protection.

Government policy towards benefit claimants works in a similar way. Most claimants are in work – either precarious, part-time employment or a full-time job in which the pay is so low that they do not have enough to live. In these circumstances state benefits operate as a subsidy to the employer, who is able to pay people less that the legitimate value of their work in the knowledge that the state will make up the difference. The political narrative, however, ignores this subsidy, focusing instead on "benefit scroungers" – a catch-all category that conflates people who defraud or otherwise exploit the system with legitimate claimants whose only offence is to be disabled, out of work or poorly paid.

Since, however, the government's own figures show that fraud accounts for 0.7% of the benefits budget – much, much less that the sum of legitimate benefits that go unclaimed – the "scroungers" problem is one that it cannot actually solve. It its place it has created new categories of the "undeserving" in the form of long-term sick, disabled and unemployed people who are not trying hard enough to find work. Like punishment, this offers a quick policy win, since the solution is no longer to find people work, but merely to save public money by withdrawing their benefits. In the year to September 2013, over a million recipients were sanctioned, their benefit reduced or stopped for infringements of a Kafkaesque set of procedural rules exploited by staff obliged to meet managerial "expectations". If people then give up on the system because it treats them so poorly, they may be directed to food-banks and homeless shelters, but government scores a further win because they are no longer counted as unemployed.

CREATING A PROBLEM it can solve in order to cover up an underlying failure is one of the most common ways in which established power entrenches a failed status quo. Across the world governments rail against (some or all of) "anti-social elements", "terrorists", "foreign interference", "spies", "conspiracies", "criminals", "religious extremists", "fascists", etc., to deflect attention away from their own shortcomings, engender fear and rally popular support. Britain is by no means immune from this tendency, even if the specific threats seem more parochial. By talking up issues such as drugs, crime, benefit fraud and immigration purely in terms of public harm, rather than seeking to expose and address the underlying human realities, government closes off the routes towards lasting solutions, the routes out of the blind alley that lead back on to the highway of authentic social and economic progress.

At the heart of this is the question of leadership, and whether it aims to collude with or challenge the failed assumptions that perpetuate the status quo. The cycle of democracy – and the news cycle that feeds it – is too short to pay attention to sustained outcomes; it is always looking forward to the next opinion poll, the next election, the next news bulletin or print deadline, where the eye-catching policy initiative and promise of action will have most impact. It is a weak democracy when the popular will is so easily hijacked; if the easiest way to win over the electorate is to conjure threats and promise to tackle them, democracy will consistently reward failure over long-term achievements in social progress.

The spirit of honest political leadership is the preserve of the retired, or nearly so. When the irrepressible Kenneth Clarke, Justice Secretary from 2010-12, by which time he was 72 and had little to lose, characterised prison as "a costly and ineffectual approach that fails to turn criminals into law-abiding citizens"[1], he showed a rare willingness to lead the challenge to a discredited orthodoxy. If he was wondering how far it would take him, the answer was "not very far": his colleagues in government reverted by default to the collusion model, he was obliged to qualify his words and was soon demoted to a lesser role. What is remarkable, however, is that such a slight and reasoned challenge should stand out as almost the only recent glimmer of enlightenment in the enveloping darkness of fearful conformity.

No sound-bite in recent decades more aptly captures the failure of political leadership to embrace the human desire for social advancement than that of British prime minister John Major, who said in 1993 in the context of child offending that "society needs to condemn a little more and understand a little less"[2]. With this he took the language of politics to new depths of truth-scrambling generalisation, whereby people were invited to ignore at their convenience everything important about their basic humanity. Understanding is an act of will, something that requires effort, determination and engagement. Condemnation, on the other hand, is easy, a futile formulation providing rhetorical cover for powerlessness and fear.

Enlightened leadership is rooted in qualities central to human experience, such as compassion, empathy, tolerance and a desire to understand rather than dictate. True to form, Mr Major's enthusiasm for human understanding returned in retirement. In a speech in 2013, with the wisdom of a seventy year-old, he launched an impassioned plea on behalf of the "millions and millions" of overlooked, financial-

---

1   Speech at the Centre for Crime and Justice Studies, London, 30 June 2010
2   *Mail on Sunday* 21 February 1993

ly insecure "dignified poor or near-poor", whose continued existence shamed decades of politicians, including himself. "For too many of these people," he said, "a room with a view is 30 stories up and every day they wake up hoping that the lift will work and that the graffiti on the walls won't be too vile."

In so speaking, this career politician, who rose from humble beginnings through a string of government appointments to a seven year stint in the highest political office in the land, neatly illustrated how incomplete is the process of western democracy. It has given people a vote, but it has neutralised that vote by breaking the connection between what people really want and need in order to flourish and what politicians are able or willing to do for them. The frustration is on both sides. The forces of continuity within politics and the economy are so powerful that the will to change is rarely sufficient to overcome them, and Mr Major was not the first, nor the last, to allude to it. Tony Blair's sometimes controversial attempts to "get things done" while prime minister have been well documented; U.S. presidents typically have a short window, assuming a compliant Congress, to pursue a distinctive agenda, before relapsing into crisis management, reacting to events and trying to keep the show on the road. In Italy, the Five Star movement won a quarter of the popular vote in the 2013 general election, but declined to enter coalition government because of the institutional forces of stasis and reaction that were ranged against their programme of fundamental social change. Following the election in Britain in 2010, the Liberal Democrats jumped the other way: having yearned for power for so long, this party of radicals became junior partner in a conservative coalition, rapidly losing a large section of their traditional support.

Politicians in government may be frustrated, but to understand the reason they need listen only to their own voices. They have surrendered economic controls to the overwhelming vested interests of "the market", which they constantly praise; they have promised people what they cannot have, offering low taxes in the same breath as high quality services that low taxes cannot pay for; they have told people that "prison works", then have neither made prisons more effective nor promoted the alternatives forms of sentencing that are known to work better; they have pursued a vociferous and punitive "war on drugs" that they know to be harmful; they have condemned benefit fraud when they know that there is hardly any; they have whipped up anti-immigrant sentiment when they know that low wage immigrant labour drives large parts of the economy; they have pledged to solve the housing crisis while implementing policies to keep house prices rising... the list is almost endless, showing not that politicians are inveterate liars but that weak, centralised democracy is a habitat in which the truth cannot thrive.

Both truthfulness and, no less important, the capacity to hear the truth are personal characteristics that live in the individual will. The political face-off between an institutionally rigid establishment tied to its commercial interests and a social culture of dependency and entitlement is a failed dialogue from which the individual will has been excluded. Neither side is listening, both sides are looking out for themselves and the truth – about what people really want and need from their government and what a government is capable of providing – has no voice in the debate.

To overcome this failure, the rising tide of institutionalisation and centralised control must be reversed, to allow a much closer connection between people and the political outcomes that they seek. Governments need to give up trying to manage everything, and people need to give up expecting them to do so. The result will be a messier politics, in which things that go wrong do so quickly and obviously, directions are changed, compromises reached, opinions altered and realities faced up to, but it will also be more *responsive* – hearing the voice of the individual more effectively and creating the collaborative frameworks that can improve the quality of people's lives.

Symptomatic of the problem is the way in which true localism has been ripped out of British politics. Local authorities have become agencies of centralised power, with increasingly little control over either the funds that they raise or the way that they spend them. The greatest loss lies at the lowest level, closest to individual people, where parish and town councils have been divested of any mean-ingful authority to direct their community's affairs. It is argued that such bodies do not have the resources or skills to be effective; that the closer decision-making is brought to the people most concerned, the greater is the scope for factionalism, entrenched disagreement and all that messiness that arises when people seek a shared way for-ward. Compared to this, the detached impartiality of a remoter body is deemed to be preferable.

The counter-argument is that only when people truly have respon-sibility over their own lives do they rise to the challenge of exerting it. People will participate constructively in town and parish politics if they know that decisions can be made and acted upon directly, that the consequences can be assessed swiftly and the direction of policy adjusted appropriately. The connection between the expenditure of effort and money, and the benefit that flows from it to the people in the community, should be clearly visible; communities that control their own budgets have a strong incentive both to weigh their deci-sions and to monitor the outcomes. For centuries, local populations were largely dependent upon their own resources, and if politics is to become more responsive the conditions must be created for the skills that underpin community autonomy to be relearned.

National politics has de-legitimised taxation, characterising it as a burden, associating it with waste and fraud, and persistently devalu-ing the services it pays for by trying to obtain them ever more cheaply. To recover the impulse towards social cohesion that taxation repre-sents, a much clearer link is needed between the individual contribu-tion made and the shared benefit derived. Hypothecated taxation, which ties specific taxes to specific spending, can assist with this. Among the best-known examples is the "road fund licence", which, for a brief period in the early 20th century, tied vehicle excise duty to road-building and repair. 80 years later British people still think of the "road tax" in this way, indicating the power of hypothecation to engage the sense of contributing. People like to know what they are buying: the idea that the National Health Service is "free" is a big part of the problem of persuading people to pay for it through general taxation. Similarly, local government provides a string of "free" services, such as waste collection, of which the usefulness is self-evident, but there is little connection made between the expense incurred and the local taxes that, in theory, are supposed to pay for them.

Almost universally, governments resist hypothecation because the transparency and accountability that comes with it offers a direct challenge to their controlling instincts. It is only by surrendering that control, however, that space can be freed-up for the social innovation that progress demands. To paraphrase Mr Major, "society needs to be trusted a great deal more and managed a great deal less"; real human progress will not be possible until governments get out of the habit of deciding what is good for people and let them work it out for themselves.

Chapter 14

THE MYTH OF WESTERN EXCEPTIONALISM

Barriers to human progress on the world stage

IN AUGUST 1941, British Prime Minister Winston Churchill and U.S. President Franklin D. Roosevelt, meeting for the first time in New-foundland, issued a joint declaration that came to be known as the Atlantic Charter. Its immediate purpose was pragmatic, intended by Roosevelt to ensure that Britain's war aims did not include the ter-ritorial extension of her empire, and by Churchill to tie America into the British war effort. Its language, however, was that of high princi-ple, identifying a series of fundamental freedoms to which the Anglo-American post-war order would adhere.

Chief of these was the right of self-determination, described as "the right of all peoples to choose the form of government under which they will live". In addition were listed: the freedom to trade, including equality of access to raw materials; economic collabora-tion, "with the object of securing for all improved labour standards, economic advancement, and social security"; "freedom from want and fear"; freedom "to traverse the high seas and oceans"; and free-dom from "the crushing burden of armament". Over the next four years the Charter was adopted by a further 45 states or governments in exile in a joint *Declaration by United Nations* and, as such, is the precursor document to the modern U.N.

Britain in 1941 was still an imperial power, accustomed to taking the long view. It differentiated its colonial overlordship from that of tyranny and exploitation by assuming obligations and responsibili-ties derived from the "Whig" view of history, according to which the self-determination of peoples would be an outcome of a gradual but inevitable progression towards enlightened liberal democracy on the British model. The progress of history takes its time, however, while the world was in a hurry. After 1945 Kipling's image of *The White Man's Burden* was effaced by the ethnic, tribal, nationalist, religious and ideological differences that consumed a rapidly de-colonising world.

The image faded, but the global aspirations of the western powers endured. In addressing his poem of 1899 to the U.S. upon its inheriting the colonial administration of the Philippines following the Spanish-American War, Kipling's foresaw how the mantle of exceptionalism – the perceptions of distinctiveness, superiority and immunity that have characterised the self-belief of powerful states through history – would extend beyond Britain in the coming century to embrace the English speaking world. It was in this spirit that the right to self-determination, so central to the founding story of the United States, should be interpreted; for when, in 1947, Roosevelt's successor, President Truman, set out the foreign policy doctrine that bears his name, he left the world in no doubt as to the direction that nations were expected to determine for themselves. "Totalitarian regimes imposed on free peoples," he asserted, "... undermine the foundations of international peace and hence the security of the United States. ... It must be the policy of the United States to support free peoples who are resisting attempted subjugation by armed minorities or by outside pressures." In so speaking he set the stage for the Cold War, an ideological confrontation in which the U.S. and its western allies competed with the Communist powers for influence in every corner of the globe.

Truman's doctrine was not so much a statement of policy as an assumption of the obligations and responsibilities with which Britain had come to characterise its imperial mission. It has its origin in a request from Britain that the U.S. take over the supply of economic and military aid to the Greek government, then engaged in civil war against Communist-backed forces. In a moment of powerful symbolism, a bankrupt Britain gratefully held out the baton of global leadership, and a resurgent United States, instead of reverting to its pre-war isolation, stood forth to receive it on behalf of "the west". In referencing "the security of the United States", however, Truman gave notice that, when the chips were down, the march of human progress would invariably give way to American self-interest.

The chips were laid down in most uncompromising fashion when the Islamic jihadist group al Qaeda flew two airliners into the World Trade Centre in New York, killing 3,000 people on 11th September 2001. Within a few days of 9/11, U.S. President George W. Bush declared "war on terror" and refocused the west's military and technical capability into a response of overwhelming force. The question was, whom to overwhelm? Modern jihadism had been born in Afghanistan to resist the Soviet invasion in 1980. The west had supported that resistance from afar, but now turned aggressor in the "graveyard of empires", fighting an asymmetric campaign that pitched its high-tech but conventional military forces against small, low-tech but agile groups of highly motivated guerilla fighters.

The Afghan war was unwinnable in the traditional sense. With its central government so weak, and little prospect of replacing it with anything much stronger, it could not provide a clean victory to atone for the outrage of 9/11. Attention turned to Iraq, a serial troublemaker with whom the west had unfinished business after the Kuwait invasion. The government of Saddam Hussein was thought to be active in "state-sponsored terrorism" and was said to have access to chemical, biological and even nuclear weapons that could make any such attack particularly potent. President Bush and British Prime minister Tony Blair magnified the threat and egged each other on; a territorial war launched in 2003 was won within days, and the U.S. rashly claimed "Mission Accomplished". But almost immediately the asymmetry set in, local insurgents and jihadists from further afield took the war to the streets and it took another 8 years and many thousands of casualties before the west could extract itself without too much embarrassment. Meanwhile, in Afghanistan, western forces were still engaged, and when, finally, after twelve years, they departed, it looked as if conditions in that fiercely independent country would revert to much as they had been before the west's intervention.

IN THE 60 YEARS between the Atlantic Charter and the disastrous wars launched in the wake of 9/11, the west threw away a huge advantage, and nobody in power seemed to grasp how it had done so. It was not that firepower was lacking; by 1945 the arsenal of the U.S. was unmatched in its extent and sophistication, and it far outspent its rivals in the decades that followed. Clearly its opponents in Afghanistan and Iraq were no match whatsoever for its military capability; what those campaigns demonstrated, therefore, is that western weaponry on its own has limited and diminishing capacity to achieve strategic and political aims.

The writing was on the wall from an early stage. The intensity of the Cold War scramble for influence after 1945, coupled with the possibility of nuclear annihilation as the arms race hotted up, caused the west to imbue Communism with the character of an existential threat to its way of life. Throughout the Cold War it allowed that threat to dictate its agenda, consuming vast resources and energy that could have been put to more constructive use. It was not obliged to do so: its model of liberal democracy was able to embrace a broad political spectrum from which the social ideals of Communism were not necessarily excluded. It would have been sufficient to remain true to Truman's exact words, to have challenged anti-democratic forces from whatever source, while continuing to assert the principles that flowed from the Atlantic Charter. Instead, the west abandoned its historiography of human progress in favour of a much narrower ideological confrontation through which it compromised its own principles of freedom.

The U.S., in particular, in it obsession with the Communist threat, allowed the "anti-red" McCarthyist witch-hunts of the 1950s to ride roughshod over fundamental rights, while supporting and arming repressive, authoritarian states and regimes, provided they were "free" ideologically from the Communist taint. In Central and South America, the Middle East, Africa, Europe and elsewhere, the western powers shored up conservative dictatorships, helping to fend off left-leaning anti-colonial and revolutionary movements irrespective of the popular support they enjoyed. Just as the freedom of expression enshrined in the American Constitution turned out not to extend to the voicing of left-leaning sympathies, so the "free peoples" in defence of whom Truman had spoken were not necessarily entitled to choose the freedom that they favoured, and sometimes the "outside pressures" deflecting them from their path of self-determination would come from the west.

To justify this approach, the west sought to characterise the confrontation in economic terms, associating freedom not with the self-determination of the human will but with capitalist opportunity. The language of freedom was adapted effortlessly to this purpose, the expressions "free market" and "free trade" infusing the western expansionist economic and cultural model with the aura of a moral good. Capitalist ideology encouraged people to compete for individual wealth, and by associating success with hard work, rather than privileged circumstances or good fortune, it gave credibility to the idea of the "deserving" wealthy. With this perspective, the military confrontations of the Cold War, whether successful or not, could be viewed as economic opportunities, since they fed the "military-industrial complex", in President Eisenhower's evocative phrase. Investment in military technology and the purchase of weapons from privately-owned arms manufacturers was one of the few forms of government spending that conservative economic theorists were willing to endorse.

If the military outcomes of the Cold War were, at best, inconclusive, the economic victory was overwhelming. Having out-produced the Communist system by far, it was no surprise that the collapse of the Soviet Union at the end of the 1980s should be seen in the west as the triumph, less of freedom over oppression, as of liberal economics over central planning. When China, also, embraced the free market system, the west's faith in the ideological freedoms of the market economy appeared completely vindicated. To demonstrate the point, powerful oligarchies of the ultra-wealthy emerged in former Communist states, ready to appropriate and exploit their countries' natural and human resources, while western consumer brands and investment poured in, embedding capitalist, free market principles ever more deeply in the global economy.

At the time of its triumph, however, the west struggled to keep up with the changes it had precipitated. Its prosperity in the post-war period derived from the huge productive advantage of its industry. The oil shock of the 1970s provided a salutary reminder of how resource dependent this was, and now the emphasis shifted again, away from production itself towards the profitable opportunities presented by global trade. The North American Free Trade Area came into being in 1994 and the World Trade Organisation was launched in the following year to reduce cross border impediments to trade and commerce. The largest trading bloc, the European Union, had twelve member states at the beginning of the 1990s, admitted three more in that decade and a further thirteen subsequently as it embraced its newly liberated eastern neighbours.

As trade increased, productive industries across the west were closed down, their activities reassigned to the cheap, abundant labour that could be harnessed in the new factories of China, south east Asia and Central and South America. In an increasingly globalised economy, the market was rampant; social cohesion suffered as the interests of labour and capital moved further apart. Privatisation of hitherto public services became the norm and national and cultural distinctiveness became secondary to the interests of multi-national companies, their global brands, the free flow of capital investment and the capacity to compete in the global marketplace. Having characterised freedom ideologically in market terms, the west had no defence against a global economy in which capital flowed freely into the hands of already-wealthy investors, leaving its formerly prosperous producers trailing in their wake.

Even the loss of its military rivals was confusing. After 1990 the west had no natural predators, but without a specific threat to its interests it appeared uncertain what to do. Obliged to assume the role of global policeman, it reaped few political dividends either in Kuwait, the liberation of which from its Iraqi occupiers left a legacy that a decade of sanctions and aerial supervision did little to resolve, or in Somalia, where the failure of U.S. humanitarian intervention culminating in the "Blackhawk Down" incident was instrumental in the decision not to try to halt the 1994 genocide in Rwanda. Intervention in the wars that dismembered the former Yugoslavia did eventually help to pacify that region, although the record of hesitation and uncertainty, characterised by disastrous episodes such as the Srebrenica massacre, clearly illustrated the limits of western willingness to engage.

Fifteen year later, and ten years into the "global war on terror", the west's attempts to influence events in Tunisia, Libya, Egypt, Yemen, Bahrain, Syria, Ukraine and elsewhere have been almost painful to witness. When the Arab Spring kicked off in Tunisia, France, its main western ally, initially offered security assistance to the corrupt police state presided over by President Ben-Ali. Only as social media brought details of large, articulate protests being violently put down did liberal-minded westerners make common cause with the protestors and France rapidly switch sides. Similarly, the Gaddafi regime in Libya in 2011 suited the west, which had worked hard to rebuild relationships after a difficult period in the 1980s and '90s; the country's oil reserves made it an important trading partner and Gaddafi was shaping up as a useful ally in the "war on terror". When, however, it became clear that a popular uprising in eastern Libya would face savage reprisals, western public opinion became engaged, the British and French governments read the runes and rushed heroically to the rescue.

The intervention in Libya turned what would have been a one-sided massacre into a more equal fight. By thus prolonging the war it probably caused more deaths than it saved, but opinion in the west is nothing if not fair-minded, and what set the western news agenda was the human story of freedom-loving individuals standing up to a dictatorial regime. In Egypt and Bahrain, also, western opinion favoured the protesters; governments preached moderation and restraint but took no steps that could jeopardise their good relations with long-standing regimes with which the U.S. in particular had close military and diplomatic ties. Three years later, the public in the west had long lost interest; Libya was at risk of fracturing at the hands of political and regional factions and had become a fertile ground for jihadist attacks; Egypt's brief flirtation with popular democracy was over and the military were *de facto* back in charge; and the U.S. fifth fleet still rode at anchor at it base in Bahrain, where Saudi Arabian forces had rescued the ruling minority from a popular revolt.

Syria was different; here, parallels were drawn with the deposed Iraqi regime of Saddam Hussein and, when civil war broke out, there were powerful voices in the U.S., Britain and elsewhere favouring a military intervention. Russia supported the incumbent regime, and although the Cold War might be over the instinct to challenge any Russian bid for influence was deep-seated. The public mood, however, turned against it, perhaps suspicious that enthusiasm for military intervention was more political than humanitarian, and reflecting a recognition that the west could no more – and no more easily – control the outcome of conflict than they had in Iraq of Afghanistan. A vote in the House of Commons killed off the adventure; the west might regret this deadliest and most brutal of recent wars, but without an effective strategy for ensuring that what emerged from the conflict would be both stable and more to its taste, it was forced to accept that there was not much it could do about it.

This powerlessness was further illustrated when Russia took advantage of a political vacuum in Ukraine to engineer a takeover of Crimea, a Russian-speaking province that was host to its Black Sea fleet. The Russians wanted the Crimea like a piece on a chessboard; the west, which for decades has been playing the pieces at the other end, didn't want them to have it, even though the doctrine of self-determination might suggest that they should. The west, however, could not resist picking sides; having assisted at the popular ousting of the Russia-leaning President Yanukovych in Kiev it was committed to supporting the government that replaced him, while cranking up the rhetoric against the Russian-backed protesters who seized local power in Ukraine's eastern regions. This provocation by Russia, manipulating local sentiment to destabilise the Kiev government, was little different to what the U.S. got up to in Central and South American states during the Cold War period. If, for the U.S., everything south of the Rio Grande is its backyard, for Russia, the Ukraine is more like the front room on its western aspect, of which it had political control since the early 18th century.

THE INCOHERENCE OF the west's response in all these situations is rooted in a tension, which developed almost immediately after 1945, between what the west said and even believed that it stood for, and what it actually did in its actions to defend its self-interests. The Atlantic Charter and its successor documents stood for self-determination, equality and freedom on an individual, human level, and the west justified its sense of exceptionalism by insisting that it subscribed to and promoted these values. But most of what it did after 1945 was intended to prioritise not those values but its own self-interest, security and wealth. Just as, in domestic policy, the status quo has become the default policy setting of established political elites, so in international affairs the primary objective has been to keep anything from happening that would threaten the west's dominant economic model.

One consequence of this approach has been the way in which the west has repeatedly surprised itself with its own failings, having too little experience of seeing any situation from the other person's point of view. It comes from viewing countries as pawns in a chess game, rather than societies of real people; if the urban elites that formed the government of South Vietnam welcomed U.S. intervention, it did not follow that rural peasant farmers would do so, although this was the group most affected by warfare and upon whom success or failure in the Vietnam War would ultimately depend. The U.S. knew far too little about the Vietnamese people, and not much more, it would seem, about those of Castro's Cuba, who failed spectacularly to rise up and support the U.S. sponsored "Bay of Pigs" invasion in 1961. Forty-two years later, as their tanks rolled into Iraq for the second time in a decade, U.S., British and allied forces expecting to be feted as liberators continued to be sorely disabused. They took no account of a history of western exploitation, still less of the racial, cultural and religious identification of this predominantly Arab people with the unresolved plight of their Palestinian cousins, for which the west is held largely to blame.

The post-war west has lost touch with the idea of history as a multi-dimensional narrative; that in the slowly developing linearity

called "progress", the place of different nations, cultures and societies varies in ways that are beyond anyone's power to control. Law
that is acceptable in one place is inhumane in another, and a form
of government that would be deemed repressive in the context of
a functioning democracy appears reassuringly strong among a people habituated to instability. Religion and culture are still powerful
forces in this respect. It should be clear, for example, that although
there have been signs of a gradual shift in Saudi Arabia towards recognising what would, in the west, be regarded as basic human rights
for women (the right to drive a car, for example), the actual status of
those rights, and the rate of progress towards increasing them, has no
connection to the western ideal.

The approach of western governments has been to challenge human
rights abuses when it suits its other policy agendas, and to ignore
them when it does not. Saudi Arabia is an important western ally, so
its approach to women's rights does not make diplomatic waves; in
Iraq and Afghanistan, on the other hand, developing women's rights
was a big issue during the periods of greatest western influence.
Those rights, however, are receding rapidly now that western influence is in decline, and in the case of Iraq are now less well developed
than they were under the more secular government of Saddam Hussein. History is unforgiving of governments that blunder into human
rights questions out of political self-interest. It is legitimate for critics
to urge faster progress, but the call must originate with the community affected. Outsiders should make common human cause with
such communities, fostering the dialogue from which may grow a
deeper-rooted process of cultural change.

In considering its progressive policy objectives, the west should
recall that, of every conceivable offence against humanity and the
rule of law to be found in the contemporary world, there is scarcely
one that it has not at some point outdone in seeking to apply its religious convictions, or in pursuit of its naked self-interest. If nobody
forgets the Spanish Inquisition, do people really know anything of
the barbaric tortures, live burnings, mass expropriations and expul-
sions practised throughout Europe in the name of differing versions

of Christianity? The activities of the Royal Navy in the Napoleonic period are the stuff of serial best-sellers, in which flogging with the cat o' nine tails is standard fare, but do people contemplate the awful reality of a punishment, which, routinely practised into the late 19th century, would tear the skin from a man's back and continue to attack the raw flesh exposed beneath it? Death by stoning may still be a feature of Sharia law, but do people remember that the pillory was used in Britain until the early 19th century, and that people sentenced to stand there frequently died slowly under a hail of missiles? "Cowboys and Indians" were a Hollywood staple in the mid 20th century and the theme of playground games that effectively sanitised the grim reality, that an indigenous population originally of many millions was close to being eliminated through violence and disease by the end of the 19th century. This was no accident or "collateral damage": as early as the 1760s the British commander Lord Amherst promoted the distribution of smallpox-infected blankets among native American communities as an effective way of reducing their numbers.

The west has normalised all these barbarities. The unpardonable detail – of genocides across America and Australasia, of slave trading on an industrial scale, of cruel and vengeful punishments, of the treatment of so-described witches, heretics, religious non-conformists, free thinkers and many others – is romanticised into the rich tapestry of history's grand themes. Punishments in the Royal Navy were not different to those elsewhere in 18th century Britain; religious persecutions were common across pre-enlightenment Europe; colonial warfare, and the casual, exploitative racism that accompanied it, were the normal ways of doing business. And it is true that during the course of the 19th century attitudes began to change, which is why the Nazi and Stalinist atrocities of the 20th century were recognised as aberrant and acknowledged as crimes.

Progress, however, in the west as elsewhere, has been gradual and piecemeal. When African states are criticised for their anti-gay legislation, do people remember its foundations in colonial era statutes bequeathed by European nations in the 1960s; or that some of the current impetus for the hardening of this legislation is coming from well-funded conservative Christian groups in the west; or that, within recent memory, gay people in parts of the west were experiencing arrest and police harassment of a kind with which people in Uganda are still familiar?

Homosexual activity was illegal in England and Wales until 1967, and in Scotland until 1980, while in the U.S., it was not constitutionally protected until 2003, hence illegal in many states until then. Russia in 2013 might have taken note that its widely criticised legislation against propagandising homosexuality to young people was little different in spirit to what was enacted in Britain under the Thatcher government as late as 1988[1]. That 25 year interval has brought about a wholesale change in British attitudes, culminating in the Marriage (Same Sex Couples) Act 2013, while Russia is significantly behind the curve. Gay rights have developed in Britain because gay people have had the courage to come out, and other people have found, gradually, that they had nothing to fear. Criticism by western governments, vulnerable to charges of hypocrisy, could merely entrench the situation in Russia, whereas a courageous stand by individuals, both in Russia and the west, can have a much deeper effect. An athlete, for example, who boycotted the Sochi Olympics could make an impression because they made a principled stand. Unlike a government, they had something to lose, and that sacrifice is the basis for a powerful human connection.

Individual action, not state interest, lies behind the advance of human rights, from the abolition of the slave trade 200 years ago to the work of non-governmental organisations such as Amnesty International in the present day. Meanwhile, western governments still actively protect state interests at the expense of the human rights of others, including their own people. To justify the "war on terror", they talked up jihadism as a new existential threat to the west, which, because it operated with no recognised rules of engagement, was much more dangerous than a conventional enemy and could

---

1   Section 28 of the Local Government Act 1988 stated, among other things, that a local authority shall not "promote the teaching in any maintained school of the acceptability of homosexuality as a pretended family relationship".

legitimately be combatted with any means. Torture, rendition, physical and mental abuse, arbitrary arrest, imprisonment without trial, targeted killings including loss of civilian life and wholesale intrusion into people's private communications on a scale not yet fully comprehended have all been legitimised in western legal frameworks in the interests of the "security" of the west. The U.S. prison at Guantanamo Bay, where suspects have been held and reportedly tortured in captivity for years without recourse to legal process, is a temple to this new order. Just as losing the Vietnam war redoubled the efforts of the military-industrial complex to assert American ascendancy, so, the disruptive effect of the failed wars in Afghanistan and Iraq have gone a long way towards justifying the new surveillance-security complex in continuing to extend its intrusive reach.

The whiff of hypocrisy that surrounds the west's preaching to its "less enlightened" neighbours serves as a reminder that while state policy provides the accidents of history, the continuous cascade of official interventions, from wars and revolutions to the myriad minor decisions and directions with which political and administrative leaders attempt to shape people's lives, beneath these shifting sands of ambition, intrigue and influence lies a human constant, independent of politics, that drives the engine of human progress. We laud it in the roll call of great men and women – Gandhi, Mandela, Wilberforce, Mother Theresa, Florence Nightingale, Solzhenitsyn – who epitomise the moral strength of the human; but we find it daily in the people we encounter in our routine lives. That constant is the capacity that every human knows, to relate a personal experience to the situation of others. For every instance of cruelty and barbarism, voices may be heard speaking up for compassion, empathy and humane treatment, and in every place, culture and community on earth there is a preponderance of people with the capacity for moral good, able to empathise with human suffering and to seek to relieve it.

The morals, values and principles of human societies lie not in states, institutions or collectivities, nor in the acts that people carry out on behalf of these, but in people themselves. Human progress derives from dialogue and engagement; the development of social interconnectedness based on shared human values, mutuality and trust. The institutionalisation of this dialogue through the norms of international diplomacy may have the opposite effect, in which authentic human connection is squeezed out by time-honoured rituals, self-serving demands, opportunistic alliances and diplomatic posturing.

International diplomacy and state-to-state negotiations are more likely to obstruct than to promote the human development that depends upon a deepening and enriching of human relationships. Its rituals, which were forged among the shifting alliances of the monarchies of Europe, conform to the adversarial model of formalised disagreement upon which English legal systems have got fat and party politics have become so vacuous and corrupted. So entrenched have they become, that even relationships designed to be collaborative have been consumed by them. The member states of the European Union, having bound themselves with a commitment to "ever-closer union", still come to the table from a position of national self-interest, trying to differentiate their positions and squeeze marginal advantages in order to proclaim "victory" when reporting back to their domestic parliaments.

If the E.U. were a human project, in which collaboration and sharing were the unifying force, the bloated bureaucracies of inter-state negotiations would be redundant. As it is, there is no such thing as a good result in those negotiations – a result in which the measure of human benefit is at centre stage. The only outcome is mediocrity, or the descent to a lowest common denominator that has more to do with uniformity than togetherness. The European Union, at the behest of its governments, has repackaged fundamental human freedoms as economic and consumer values that are chiefly of benefit to commercial interests, who want unfettered access to markets on terms most favourable to themselves. Governments support this for reasons we know well: that the removal of market barriers increases transactional activity, which flatters the headline measure of GDP.

THE MYTH OF exceptionalism is this: that the west has convinced itself that moral and cultural ascendency is innate to its social and economic values, and that this can be preserved through the actions of government. In reality, almost the *exact opposite* is the case. Whatever claim the west may have to such ascendancy has emerged from the chance accidents of a dark and troubled history, of which the moments of brightness are in the sparks thrown up by individual acts of difference and dissent. Just as evolution depends upon the introduction of disruptive variables that are tested by nature, human progress also requires the interplay of diverse opinions, the expression of difference, the right to oppose established social and economic norms and to counter-propose alternatives from which people may choose.

An enlightened state, wishing to advance the cause of human progress, would do well to avoid moralising and let people get on with it. Instead of directing, it should apply its energies to facilitating the individual relationships and interactions that allow people to advance in mutual understanding. The modern, corporatist state, however, resists this: so protective is it of its vested interests that it curtails severely the scope of enlightened dissent. "So far, but no further," the system determines: freedom is a consumer good, no more valuable than any other, so the freedom of *difference* must not advance beyond the point at which the established institutions of society and the economy are protected. Thereafter, demonstrations must be broken up, protest groups must be infiltrated, free expression must be moderated, "terrorist" suspects must be tortured, asylum-seekers must be thrown out, benefit claimants must be stigmatised, young black people must be victimised and whole populations must be subject to the blanket oversight of their electronic communications, all in the name of a system of government that is trapped in a paradigm of institutional control.

Human rights are individual, as the Universal Declaration makes clear, but the institutionalisation and bureaucratisation of the western model of government from the Cold War to the "war on terror" has seen a steady dilution of those individual rights in favour of collective rights, which are vested in the state on behalf of its citizens. The impact upon the right to free speech, free assembly, the right to protest, the right to withdraw labour and to strike, and the right to "just and favourable conditions of work and remuneration[1]" has been severe. With the objective of protecting people from each other, British and other western governments have successively legislated to narrow the opportunities for effective dissent, asserting that the established social, political and economic model already offers an appropriate set of freedoms. The message is subtle, but pervasive, summed up in the disingenuous mantra that if you have done nothing wrong you have nothing to hide. Government has established an appropriate balance of rights, duties and freedoms, and, if you don't like it, you're a wrong'un.

Typical of this approach was the curbing of trades union and labour rights in Britain in the 1980s. While the western powers were enthusiastically supporting the Solidarity Trade Union in Communist Poland, the Thatcher government was rapidly dismantling rights painfully acquired by the labour movement in Britain over the previous hundred years. The object was to make it very much harder for workers to seek improvements to their terms and conditions by withdrawing their labour. The justification was that the withdrawal of labour was harmful to the interests of the national economy, a harm from which the generality of the population were entitled to be protected by the state. The question is: who was being protected? The evidence shows that from the time of these changes the distribution of wealth in the economy, which, over previous decades, had been becoming more equal, now began to diverge. Over the next three decades the rich got relatively richer, and in particular the senior management of large companies saw their total pay increase many, many times faster than that of the people they employ. In the same period, much skilled labour was made redundant as the manufacturing and heavy industry that had employed it was closed down.

The labour laws of the 1980s did not cause these outcomes, but

---

1   Article 23, *Universal Declaration of Human Rights*

they took away one of the human freedoms that might have countered them. "Facilitating relationships" in this context would involve removing the structural advantages of one or other side – advantages that would make it less likely that the people concerned would sit down as human equals and try to sort things out. As it is, the reforms made it easier to close businesses and encouraged employers to challenge strikes in the courts rather than through engagement with their productive workers. By curtailing the opportunity for organised dissent, the government reduced the number of variables that combine to shape the path of human progress. It is far from certain that the British economy since the 1980s has worked out in the best way that it could; if "just and favourable conditions of work and remuneration" are indeed a right that tends towards human progress, the union reforms may be seen in the light of history as a retrograde step.

More recently, the "Occupy" movement, which first came to prominence in 2011, has been subject to this limiting effect. The agenda for change of this loose, global movement is focused on rising inequality, for which it holds the dominance of large corporations in economic and political affairs mainly responsible. As its name suggests, the movement's *modus operandi* has been to place groups of protesters in highly visible places where their message would be difficult to ignore. These rendered themselves vulnerable to the exercise of "collective rights" under laws of obstruction and the protection of private property. The rights of other people to go about their (generally commercial) business and the rights of corporations and public bodies to evict people from premises they owned were set above the right to protest. Many peaceful occupations, in the U.S., Britain and elsewhere, were violently broken up by security forces or this reason.

Once again, the loss to human progress lay not in the Occupy movement being "right" or "wrong" in its analysis, but in failing to recognise that active, uncomfortable and even disruptive dissent tests a society's institutions and helps them to evolve in a progressive way. That the people of the west appeared more willing to understand this in relation to the Arab Spring protests than in relation to themselves neatly encapsulated how the myth of western exceptionalism has taken hold. Exceptionalism assumes a moral ascendancy from which others may learn; if the west does, indeed, however, have a head start in the progress of history, it arose through a capacity for *self*-improvement and *self*-learning that was boosted by the intellectual developments of the 18th century enlightenment, in which many orthodoxies were challenged. This process is very far indeed from being completed and now appears under threat.

IN THE PROJECT embarked upon by Roosevelt and Churchill at their conference in 1940, of promoting the self-determination of peoples and their fundamental freedoms, the west has given poor examples over recent decades. The incalculable sums expended to "win" the post-9/11 wars have, in fact, been calculated at something in the region of a trillion dollars, in addition to the thousands of allied servicemen and the far greater number of Iraqi and Afghans who lost their lives. The cost of the Vietnam War in today's money would be much the same, and in loss of life was far, far greater. In both cases the strategic gains were negligible and the loss of global influence considerable, while the sheer size of the numbers – the quantity of life and wealth they represent – testify to the scale of the opportunity that has been discarded, the colossal gains that could have been reaped if the west had been willing to share its advantage constructively to the benefit of all.

This opportunity is ever-present: there is no time at which the wealthy west might not choose to expend its surpluses to such enormous human benefit. In place of such sharing, however, it has sought every opportunity to make an ideological virtue out of competitive advantage, one that thrusts its tentacles into all the crevices of existence, souring relationships and showing an example to the world that is rooted in self-interest and financial greed. The world has been quick to learn: emerging economies across the globe present a rising challenge to the west's commercial hegemony, causing its policymakers to turn even further towards an increasingly paranoid language of attrition with new enemies seen at every turn. To match the wars on terror and drugs, "wars on" and "fights against" all manner of social evils have been declared, and now Britain, encumbered with an unproductive economy fuelled by unprecedented levels of consumer debt, has even succumbed to the rhetoric of a "global economic race" in which those emerging economies are its chief competitors.

A race, by definition, has winners and losers, but the result in this case means nothing in national terms. A century ago Britain was the world's pre-eminent power; for most of the post-war period it has been producing less than it consumes, bailing itself out with the proceeds of its overseas investments, and yet in 2014 it is home to more billionaires than ever in its history. Wealth is not bounded by national borders: extreme poverty is found in the wealthiest of countries, while extreme wealth is found among the poorest. The people whose lose out in the "global race" are not confined to any country but are widely distributed across the earth.

Nonetheless, within national economies the paradigm of winners and losers is deeply engrained. In Britain, "winners" own houses and "losers" do not; "winners" get into the schools of their choice and "losers" do not; "winners" have accountants to organise their tax avoidance and "losers" are accused of benefit fraud; "winners" have solid, professional jobs stirring wealth around the system and "losers" have zero-hours contracts or long hours on low pay. And all the time the system churns out the national competitive message, that Britain is a "winner" because its GDP growth is a percentage point above someone else's, whose economy is "stagnating" while Britain's, on account of it famously "flexible" workforce (low pay and zero-hours contracts), is "forging ahead"; or that Britain's "world-beating" (if productively useless) financial services industry will collapse into nothing if someone tries to tax its transactions or regulate its trades; or that Britain's children will "lose out" if they do not match those of south east Asia in international "league tables".

Those league tables are part of the problem. Nobody is innately a winner or a loser, but an education system focused on competitive advantage can rapidly make them one or the other. That is why the renewal of the cause of social progress can only start by going back to the classroom.

Chapter 15

"EXPECTED PROGRESS"

The uses and abuses of assessment in schools

IN THE MONTHS before his party was elected to government in 1997, former British prime minister Tony Blair famously described his three main priorities for government as "education, education and education". It was a memorable sound-bite that drew attention to an important truth, that most of the challenges with which society is faced have education at their root. Economic prosperity, physical and mental health, social integration and public order, the capacity and willingness of people to look after both themselves and others: all these depend greatly on behaviour, which in turn is influenced by the way in which people have been formed by society.

The government commands the productive time of every state-educated child every working day for approximately four fifths of a full working year, so the lives of schoolchildren have an overwhelming impact on the attitudes, habits and practices that are formed by successive generations as they enter the wider world. Society shapes schooling and the products of schooling shape society. This positive feedback underpins the status quo and helps to explain why education is among the most politicised areas of public administration. For a century or more, each generation has been more extensively educated, and to a higher level, than that which preceded it, giving rise to the received wisdom that parents are not qualified to decide upon the education of their children. Government has assumed that role and, as well as organising and paying for them, decides what schools should teach and how to measure their success.

This could change. With half of school leavers aspiring to a university degree, it is possible that Britain has reached "peak education" on the current model, in which case parents are likely to become increasingly outspoken on the subject of their children's schooling. For the moment, however, the established orthodoxy, in which the state provides a free school education on the government's terms, remains deeply engrained. In that speech to his party's conference in 1996, Mr Blair left no room for doubt about what those terms were. "We are 35th in the world league of education standards today," he said; "... give me the education system that is 35th in the world today and I will give you the economy that is 35th in the world tomorrow." Among the solutions he offered: "three-week intensive literacy summer schools for all those falling behind"; "continual assessment, targets set, instant action where they are not met"; "a commitment to keep costs to schools for access to the internet and superhighway as low and as predictable as possible"; "no child to be without access to a computer and no school unable to use them properly". The implication was obvious: for Blair, as for his colleagues, predecessors and successors, education is a tool to drive the economy, and society lives or dies by the success with which young people participate in the competitive, networked, global marketplace that was, and remains, the government's chosen model of progress. Physical health, social and emotional wellbeing, human relationships, happiness – indeed, almost everything that we have characterised as having human value – have, at best, occasional walk-on parts in this grand scheme.

The language is telling: "intensive" additional courses for those "falling behind"; "continual assessment"; "targets"; "instant action" for targets "not met"; it reveals the development of children reduced to numbers on a scoresheet, reproducing the stressful world of the competitive global economy in an educational framework that is competitive and stressful in its own right. In Britain's schools, nearly a fifth of eleven year-olds were obese in 2013. They will carry this condition into adulthood, where the primary causes of premature death – heart, lung and liver disease, and acts of self-harm – are closely related to socially conditioned outcomes and behaviours such as poverty, inadequate housing, poor diet, lack of exercise, abuse of alcohol and tobacco, oppressive working conditions, atmospheric pollution, greed and emotional distress. These are the side-effects and coping mechanisms connected with participation in an economy in which requiring people to work as long and hard as possible – irrespective of its usefulness – is the fastest route to GDP growth, and, therefore, government's primary objective. Schools perform a double task in this connection, since 30 sets of parents are freed to work in the money economy while a teacher endeavours to instil in their children the skills they need to join that economy in their turn.

LEARNING IS A form of work, and there is a parallel here with the three characteristics of worthwhile work described in Chapter 7 – that it should be useful, interesting and autonomous if it is to engage people effectively. Autonomy comes from learning through experience: people who learn actively, by doing things, rather than passively, by absorbing the input of others, remain in control. Interest come from a combination of feedback and motivation that keeps the learner engaged. Usefulness is central to the sense of reward: the knowledge or skill acquired assists the learner both in their own life and as a contributing member of society.

Babies learn through experiment and feedback, instinctively seeking the rewards that will keep them alive. They do stuff, they see what happens and they learn what works. Every sense is tuned to absorb as much information as possible: given the chance, young children will touch, taste, smell, listen to and observe everything within their sensory and literal reach, in search of instant feedback. The "play" of a child is a deadly serious process of self-directed learning that launches a life-long adventure in curiosity, experiment and encounter, accompanied by a gradual transition from the centre of that sensory universe to an individual's place in a more complex world of inter-relatedness.

The task of education is to guide that transition, placing the teacher in a facilitative role relative to the innate capacities of the child. Those capacities for curiosity, invention, experimentation and imagination generally flourish best in a social, collaborative context. School is the stage for an unending cycle of social experiments through which children chart their path to an awareness of the relationship of self and other, and if education is about anything it is about building integrity and respect into relationships with the world of people, things, events, emotions and ideas. How strange, therefore, that just as children are poised to face outwards to explore those relationships, all the focus in terms of their achievement and development is turned in upon a narrow range of individualised, functional goals. Much of the emphasis in classrooms is on "differentiation", or the capacity of teachers to set sufficient challenge to children of differing ability in a given task. But at no point are the children assessed as a group, on their capacity to collaborate effectively in the interests of all. So each child ploughs its solitary furrow, with a score at the end of it, while the participation for which they are yearning is pushed to the margins of the school experience.

Truly productive work demands creativity and inventiveness. Making and mending require manual dexterity, fine motor skills, hand to eye coordination, a feel for tools and materials. Designing and inventing require imagination and the curiosity that leads to experimentation. Performing, whether on stage, in a concert hall or a sports stadium requires a range of complex physical co-ordinations embracing voice, ear, hands, feet, breathing, balance, poise and agility. Writing, whether as novelist, journalist or poet, requires curiosity, inventiveness and human insight. Caring, whether for the sick, the old, the young or the disabled, requires empathy, understanding, consideration and respect. Farming requires a connection with the seasons, the weather, the soil and the lives of animals and plants. All these are the primary human attributes that have accompanied the advance of the human race over thousands of years, yet, despite their centrality to the human experience, none feature within the key measures of educational achievement set down by the government.

Backed by its regulator, Ofsted – the Office for Standards in Education, Children's Services and Skills, to give its full-blown title – government dictates the areas of attainment in which children are assessed, initially at age two to three, then again at age five and thereafter at five more "key stages", as well as numerous other assessments in between, all in relentless pursuit of "expected progress" in literacy, numeracy and information technology. If it all sounds like a military campaign, the metaphor is appropriate. With its terminology of "winning" in the "global economic race", it may not involve tanks or guns (other than those crated up to be exported) but it certainly involves footsoldiers. In the GDP economy, qualities such as inventiveness, creative problem-solving and the capacity to think "outside the box" may be highly-prized among the entrepreneurial few, but for everybody else it is the basic processing tools that are considered most important.

With their focus upon narrow, pre-defined tasks, examinations and assessments attempt to replicate the world of real work in which success is characterised by the ability to carry out detailed instructions. Results evidence a candidate's capacity to perform to order, while the knowledge acquired, particularly in the more "academic" subjects which the standards favour, rarely contributes directly to employability. Practical skills may do so – the ability to speak Spanish or Chinese would certainly have value in the right context – but here, as in every practical field, it is the ability that counts rather than the qualification. A GCSE in a modern language is no evidence of a functional skill.

This inconsistency sits at the heart of the British education system. On the one hand, all the political emphasis is on providing the skills of the workplace; on the other, the politically-inspired curriculum favours academic subjects that traditionally have been selected and taught in pursuit of an idealised "liberal education". That ideal, advanced centuries ago in the elite (and privately funded) public schools for the cultivation of young gentlemen of ample means, embraces knowledge and learning for its own sake. This tradition is stamped deep on a national school curriculum strongly influenced by government ministers and their advisers, many of whom were themselves educated in those exclusive establishments. By way of content, it features the so-called "facilitating subjects" still favoured by the elite universities to which more able school students are expected to aspire. The list is a short one; only biology, chemistry, physics, mathematics, geography, history, English literature, modern and classical languages are included.

The omissions are striking. Quite apart from the many so-called "soft" subjects, such as media and business studies, the traditional disciplines of music, art, theology and even philosophy are excluded. Practical skills, manual dexterity, emotional and social intelligence, imagination, creativity and inventiveness are completely absent. The inclusion of the dead classical languages of ancient Greece and Rome illustrates that the list has been chosen not for contemporary relevance but in pursuit of an elitism that applies the term "academic" to all that it considers worthwhile and rigorous in educational practice. To advance this cause, government policy has for decades been focused on getting as many people to university as possible. The number of first degrees awarded by UK universities for full-time courses rose from 17,000 in 1950 to 351,000 in 2011[1.] Predictably enough, however, this enormous expansion of the university sector has removed the guarantee of social and economic advancement that once it offered. For many, university has become little more than a high-cost gateway to employment that previously could be accessed through apprenticeship or on-the-job training.

ONLY A MINORITY of students can get the plum jobs, while in school only a minority of pupils can truly excel. The focus on exceptional achievement must embrace a corresponding underperformance among those who do not stand out from the crowd. In education, as with wealth and incomes, the average outcome has little to say about individual cases, the more so because in education nobody really knows where the average lies. Is a grade A in English Literature more valuable that a high-scoring BTEC in sport? Maybe, but valuable to whom? In the face of such subjectivity the term "average student" has little meaning, even though it is widely used.

---

1   Bolton P., *Education: Historical statistics*, House of Commons Library, 27 November 2012

Government overcomes this shortcoming by applying averages to
schools rather than to pupils. A threshold is set for pupil achievement, and the number of children who reach that level provides a
yardstick against which the performance of each school is measured.
The graph below charts the improvement over the previous year in
the percentage of pupils achieving five GCSEs (or equivalent) at any
grade, compared with the number achieving five GCSEs at grades
A* to C. The former group has increased very little, because, at over
90%, it had reached a natural limit. The latter group showed a steady
increase, followed by a tailing off in the rate of improvement. This
suggests that schools reacted with some success to pressure to prioritise the C grade, before another natural limit was reached. It also
shows that they could find subjects for most students at which they
could do reasonably well.[1]

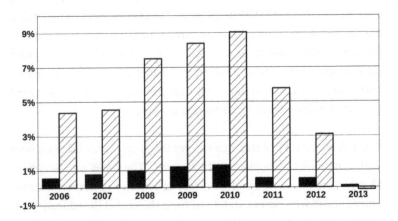

*Year on year percentage increase in the proportion of pupils achieving five or
more GCSEs at grade A*-G or equivalent (dark bars) and five or more GCSEs
at grade A*-C or equivalent (light bars). Source: Key stage 4 attainment data
(state-funded schools).*

1   Educational statistics quoted apply to England only. Education is a devolved
     power and other parts of the UK have their own systems.

Governments react to this plateau effect by raising the stakes. The next graph shows the same data for pupils achieving five GCSEs at grades A* to C including English and mathematics, compared to those achieving the EBacc performance measure, which was introduced in 2010. The former measure follows the established pattern, with improvements on a declining trend as the total reaches the 60% level. The EBacc measure, which includes pupils achieving grades A* to C in English, mathematics, history or geography, the sciences and a language, started to increase sharply in 2013, and is likely to rise further for a few more years before reaching its natural limit.

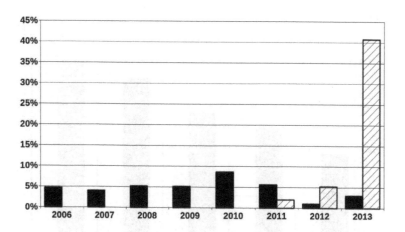

Year on year percentage increase in the proportion of pupils achieving five or more GCSEs at grade A*-C or equivalent, including English and maths GCSEs (dark bars) and the EBacc performance measure (light bars). Source: Key stage 4 attainment data (state-funded schools)

Schools did not know about the EBacc when they entered pupils for examinations in 2010, but they soon got the idea. The easiest way to demonstrate continual improvement is to target the top of the ability range, and now the government can point to a 40% increase in the number of pupils achieving the EBacc when the data for less able pupils is levelling off. The logic behind this can be seen in the third graph, which charts the pupils making "expected progress" in English and mathematics at age 16 in relation to their performance at key stage two, at the age of 11. Only 15% of those achieving level 1 (the lowest) at key stage two in mathematics have maintained that level five years later; 85% have fallen further behind. For those achieving level 5 the reverse is the case: 82% of 16 year-olds have maintained the level they achieved at the age of 11. The figures for English are less extreme, but no less striking: the lower the level at key stage two, the lower the chance of maintaining the progress that has already been made.

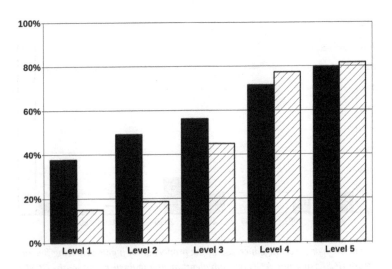

Percentage of pupils making "expected progress" in English (dark bars) and mathematics (light bars) at age 16 in relation to their performance level at age 11. Source: 2012-13 key stage 4 attainment data (state-funded schools).

Pushing higher ability groups to do even better, therefore, is a more fruitful prospect than pushing those whose starting point is nearer the bottom. For this reason, proposed changes to the threshold for 2014 will see schools assessed on the best *eight* GCSE results for each of their pupils, while practical subjects that favour the less academically gifted are being taken out of the threshold data. In the global economy, when even the performance of children in international tests is keenly contested by governments wishing to assert their credentials on the world stage, an emphasis on intellectual and "academic" achievement over practical, vocational, physical, social and emotional intelligence is a political imperative. Thresholds are a blunt instrument but they bring rapid results. Like swing voters in a handful of marginal constituencies at a general election, small changes can have a big impact on the published outcomes. The improvement of recent years may say more about the sophistication of school managers in addressing targets upon which their reputations depend than it does about the life chances of the pupils in their care, but from the point of view of government it is the numbers that talk.

EDUCATION IS FOCUSED on narrow attainment criteria in the same way that economic policy is focused on GDP, and for much the same reasons. It is easy to measure and compare progress against a single metric, and it is easier and faster to improve performance against a narrow measure of achievement. Just as transactional activity in the economy ramps up GDP much faster that real, productive work, clever management of a transactional assessment system can show rapid progress in educational attainment, irrespective of whether it addresses real human need. The failure of the economy to prioritise productive work, making and doing the things that people want and need, and the failure of the education system to prioritise the higher orders of human intellectual and emotional potential, are, therefore, closely linked. Transactional economic activity and transactional education are both allowed to displace productive activity because the system of worth that is being applied does not reflect true human value.

Process must come before outcome, and educationalists rightly identify the developmental importance of a child's earliest years. Why, therefore, do they proceed to load them with discrete tasks in literacy, numeracy and I.T., while ignoring or side-lining the developmental activity that would build capacity to perform those tasks in the future? The British education system demands measurable progress long before it has worked out where each child's distinctive set of attributes, capacities and potentials is trying to lead them. Curiosity and imagination build will and intention; physical co-ordination develops intellectual agility; social interaction builds shared purpose. Exploration, experimentation and self-expression are directed not at task-fulfilment but at instilling the motivational habits that encourage children to grow into life-long learners.

Building motivation is the most neglected aspect of this outcomes-focused system, in which the aspirations of high-achievers are distorted and those of low achievers are rarely accounted for. With eleven years of schooling between the reception class and the GCSE year, the 40% or so of pupils who emerge below (and often well below) the main GCSE threshold are an indictment of the system, not because it has failed to teach them what they need to pass, but because it has failed to identify, develop and validate the talents that they brought with them to school at the age of four or five. It is doubtful, however, whether the high achievers are much better served: by buying into a system of progression that leads through the key stages to GCSEs, "A" levels and a university place, they are driven as much by fear of economic and social failure as by their authentic aspirations and desires. In both cases there is wastage: one group is misdirected towards failure; the other group is required to perform tasks to demonstrate a capacity they already have. Either way, much more fundamental aspects of child and adolescent development are neglected.

This should not be surprising. An education system geared to meeting the needs of the British economy is likely to reflect that economy in significant ways, including the colossal waste arising from a misdirection of human energy and resources. Most notably, the system is highly unequal: like the economy, it offers opportunities for a minority of advantaged students to do well in terms that almost guarantee them a privileged place in society – an approach justified by market theory and the belief that top-down wealth-creation is in the best interests of society as a whole. According to that theory, the system does what it is designed to do, efficiently providing the majority of young people with the skill-set required of a free market footsoldier. To achieve this, each step in educational attainment is measured with reference not to the human value it generates but to the transactional "way in" that it provides to the money economy. Thus, straight A grades at "A" level are the "cost" of an elite university education, and a good degree from an elite university is the cost of a well paid job in a city bank or law firm. People who have less of this educational currency are obliged to buy their way in at a lower level, if they can buy in at all.

Mr Blair was right, therefore, that education is central to economic and social progress, but he and his successors have been wrong in their recipe for a programme that reinforces rather than challenges society's ills. In assessing only a narrow range of intellectual achievement, that programme takes no account of human value and the social capital that arises from collaborative work. Collaboration is at the heart of a productive economy, and of a society in which all people may flourish to the greatest extent. A socially useful education would seek to develop the skills that encourage people to work effectively together in a collaborative way. Whereas examining, grading, setting and even social mobility itself produce a distribution of success and failure, a social, collaborative education is universal, since success is shared. The benefit is two way: collaboration heightens inventiveness, extends possibilities and provides social incentives; thus, people do better together as the success of each individual makes a valued contribution to the whole.

WHEN IT COMES to political, social and economic change, knowing what is wrong is not enough, for the signs are there for all to see. The question is how to challenge an established order that is so entrenched. It arises not because there is a rich, powerful minority protecting its vested interests against a subservient majority: that might pose some practical problems but the procedure for addressing it would, in principle, be straightforward. It arises because there is a large, and largely passive, majority so internally conflicted about its interests, purpose, aspirations and direction – and so accepting of its circumstances – that it has lost the power to take decisive action that could lead to change.

We live in a dictatorship of self-imposed conformity, of which education provides the clearest example. State schools exist in a hermetic system in which government provides the money, decides what is done with it and backs this up with a powerful inspection network. Parents are obliged to send their children to school and are fined if they don't; schools that Underperform are merged or closed down; everybody within that system knows what they have to do to survive; results and outcomes follow directives with remarkable speed. It justifies itself by producing more GCSE and "A" level passes at higher grades and in subjects associated with traditional standards, and more university degrees at the end of it. Nobody questions whether these are the results to which the system should be aspiring, or that society needs.

So inflexible a regime might be defended if the results were truly as impressive as they are made to appear. By 2013, 70% of 16 year-old pupils had made the progress expected of them when assessed at the age of eleven. This figure increased rapidly from 2006 as schools adjusted to the assessment system, before approaching its natural plateau. Good though it may sound, it means that nearly one in three pupils in the state system are regressing relative to expectation during the crucial years in which they are preparing to face out to the world. Underperforming eleven year-olds are much more likely to regress, as we have seen, so the gap in performance between higher and lower achievers increases markedly as they approach adult life. But every ability range is affected: one in five of the best performing eleven year-old pupils regressed, the percentage making better than expected progress was negligible and for each level of expected progress the highest concentration of pupils was at the bottom end of the acceptable range.

Poor reading, writing and mathematics skills need be no great handicap to a ten year-old, but by the age of 16 they really matter. So the system has convinced itself that the way to improve 16 year-old outcomes is to apply more academic rigour in the earlier years. The primary schools have got the message; in 2013 about 90% of eleven year-old pupils had made the progress expected of them from the age of seven. This figure has also risen, although not as rapidly because it had less far to go; younger children given closer personal attention in smaller schools were already doing well in their assessment tasks. It is no surprise that, in general, they are more accepting of their circumstances and more willing to conform and apply themselves than their older siblings in much larger, more impersonal schools.

Improvement in set tasks at an early age, however, does not necessarily translate into better long term outcomes. If 100% of pupils were to arrive at secondary school having made expected progress in the previous four years, it might simply mean that more of them would have further to fall. The objective should be to send pupils on their journey ready to accelerate, but instead they slow down; so the targets primary schools are meeting are clearly not the ones that the children need. Secondary schools talk of having to play catch-up with pupils who are inadequately prepared, but what if the preparedness they truly lack is mental, psychological, emotional and social, rather than in traditional "academic" skills? They might not mind if pupils came to them ill-informed, provided they were healthy, self-confident, emotionally mature, quick-witted, creative and raring to learn.

Targets, goals and objectives are essential in any sort of social project; people cannot work together unless they know what they are trying to achieve. When objectives are not stated or are ill-defined they have a tendency to emerge from generalised or tacit assumptions. The assumption that literacy, numeracy and the data-processing skills that pave the way for academic study are the essential goals of a child's education is rarely challenged for this reason. Yet few teachers consider that having the most tested children in the western world focusing from an early age on a narrow skill set, and with no formal requirement to develop practical, emotional, creative and physical skills, is a good idea. Unable to perform that facilitative role of which we spoke, they are required instead to demonstrate with evidence that each lesson is contributing to pupil progress as measured by government-defined achievement criteria. The administrative and bureaucratic burden is immense, with primary school teachers reporting a 60 hour working week, of which 19 hours are spent actually teaching.[1] Head teachers, managers and school governors are torn between providing children with the education that will allow them to flourish and satisfying the regulatory framework. They know, however, that while the former is an aspiration, the latter is not optional, so the framework comes first.

What of children and their parents? The people most entitled to be concerned by the nature of school education have a limited voice. For children, school is like any new experience: they apply to it their innate learning techniques of experiment, observation and feedback. At the age of five, or seven, or even eleven, they go to school in anticipation of the relationships they will negotiate during the course of the day with their peers and teachers. "Academic" learning takes place in so far as those relationships demand it. Children may wish to satisfy their teachers or keep up with their friends; or they may wish to oppose their teachers and play games with their friends. Either way, they respond emotionally rather than judgmentally to whatever school throws at them, finding it either a good or a bad experience depending upon the relationships they form.

Parents know this. What they tend to want is for their children to be happy. Government compiles performance tables based on certain criteria to assist them in their judgement, but happiness is not one of them. Nearly everything they will hear from schools concerns either the extent to which their children are making "expected progress" in key subjects, or their level of attendance. In this way the system co-opts parents to its own targets and instils a culture of success or failure in their minds. Nobody wants their child to fail, so parents buy in to the system, only questioning the approach the school is taking when the results are not good.   ·

Children accept; parents buy-in; teachers do what they are told; school leaders give the orders and governing bodies hold them to account for their school's performance in the rankings. Everybody is complicit in an education system that breeds inequality and in which

---

1   *Teachers' workload diary survey 2013* , DfE February 2014

children, on average, Underperform; because the lower achievers Underperform so much more than the higher achievers, pupils leaving school are significantly less equal than when they entered it at the age of five. The effect continues from the moment they become active in the real-world economy, which extends and reinforces the inequalities of the school system while confirming the expectations that the school years have instilled. The narrow, competitive assessment system that schools are required to operate provides a self-fulfilling prediction of how children will fare in adult life.

Everybody knows this, and yet few are asking how it could be different; how differentiation in teaching could be tasked with recognising and developing authentic human diversity, allowing all children to flourish instead of marking their relative success or failure on a single, linear scale. Few are asking, and yet such change is entirely possible. Government ministers have it in their power to direct the way in which schools are assessed, and it is perfectly feasible to measure pupil progress in tasks and situations designed to develop collaborative working, problem-solving capacity, inventiveness, empathy, motivation and self-esteem, as well as in specific areas of knowledge and practical skills. The effect of doing so would be transformative both of educational outcomes and the social and economic expectations that prevail in adult life.

AFTERWORD

The elephants in the room

IN A FUNCTIONING democracy, there is nothing to be overthrown other than our expectations and assumptions about what we want our politics to achieve. Ultimately we get what we vote for, but the limits to our aspirations have been carefully nurtured by politicians, economists, big corporations, newspaper and television journalists and their proprietors, all acting in the interests of established power. Changing expectations is the central theme of human politics: moving from the assumption that life must be a competitive struggle to one in which people work collaboratively to maximise human value requires that people see how reasonable an expectation this is. Just as the "expected progress" of a child's school years should relate to fundamental human attributes, so people should expect and intend that society organise itself in whatever way best contributes to collective wellbeing, so that all people may flourish.

Expectation, however, is our ally in this struggle. Public administration is the pursuit of the measurable, expressed in goals and targets in which expectations have been embedded. We need only to adjust those expectations for policy to change. We hail it as a success that in Britain in 2014 more paid hours were being worked than at any time in recorded history, despite the fact that people's incomes were falling in real terms so they needed to work harder and harder to make ends meet. Paid hours and the profits to be generated from them translate into GDP growth, which is almost the sole object of economic policy; from a time, decades ago, when the wages of one full-time worker could sustain a family, it now takes the wages of two – a situation that has nothing to do with liberating women from hearth and home and everything to do with the vast amount of additional, unproductive work generated by an economy that is targeted at an inappropriate measure. If, instead, we embed the expectation of human value into goals and targets, the wheels of the policy machine will be redirected towards outcomes of collective social benefit.

Environmental wealth – the air we breathe, the water we drink, the land we live on, cultivate and enjoy – is a large component of human value. Most of the things that we want and need in life are dependent upon it. Climate change is affecting the way in which those resources are used, and will do so much more as rainfall patterns are disrupted, sea levels rise and populations are displaced from previously fertile soils and inundated coastlines. Elsewhere, synthetic chemicals pervade soil, plant and river life, disrupting natural cycles such as pollination and the animal food chain, while in some cities the air is so laced with pollutants that it is dangerous to breathe. Economic activity is largely to blame, and in valuing the growth implied by that activity we fail to account for the losses experienced by the many victims of environmental degradation.

This is why the environment is the elephant in the room where any discussion of the economy is taking place. What sense does it make to talk up growth if our activities are threatening the capacity of the earth to support human life? Conventional responses have focused on the material aspects of existence: recycling to consume less, and developing technologies such as clean energy that reduce the harms caused. The key term is sustainable, which describes a material impact with no long-term associated harm, but the word can equally be applied in a social context. Sustainable relationships are ones that do not self-destruct; that are built on mutuality of interests, freedom of participation and equality of engagement, so neither party tries to gain specific advantage.

A society that prioritises sustainable relationships through its politics automatically addresses environmental concerns, both in relation to the impact upon the earth and the way that humanity is able to adjust to it. An economy directed at maximising human value will be much less wasteful both of work and resources. By encouraging robust, locally productive communities and eliminating much transactional activity there will be fewer offices and shops to be heated and cooled, less travel required for commuting and business meetings and fewer goods shifted long distances around the world, all of which will make a difference to the volume of carbon dioxide being pumped into the atmosphere. Climate change, however, is less of a threat than the way in which people react to it. There are very few challenges that cannot be solved when the will and the purpose of a group are combined to address them; but so long as the system negates that, encouraging people to seek profit from the condition of others, no amount of ingenuity can withstand its corrosive force.

Collaborative economics, therefore, represent not so much a theoretical ideal as an existential necessity; the survival of the human race depends upon its capacity to create institutional structures that reflect the mutually supportive relationships that people naturally form. For that reason, the other elephant in the room, much bigger and much less talked about even than the environmental question, represents the 50% of the population the voice of whom is so little heard wherever political, economic and administrative decisions are made. It is not too much to say that women are excluded, marginalised or under-represented in public affairs precisely because they would not, if they could change it, tolerate the state of affairs with which humanity is confronted. The full participation of women on equal terms and in equal numbers is essential, therefore, if mutually supportive social structures are to become the norm.

THE PARADIGM SHIFT in human history that was triggered by developments in Britain in the latter half of the 18th century, the first such since the birth of civilisation six thousand years ago, is already due to be eclipsed now that the forces that unleashed the industrial revolution have done their work. The conditions for the next shift are already upon us. In the 21st century there are scarcely any technological limits on production; the problem is no longer how to produce wealth, but how to distribute it, acknowledging the absurdity of competing for something that could be so abundant. For it is now only the hoarding of wealth that keeps so many in conditions of poverty.

Once again, Britain is in the vanguard of change – a country of immense wealth but mounting inequality in which chronic indebtedness, poorer health outcomes, declining relative incomes and inadequate, unaffordable housing all contribute to the gradual reduction in participation in the national wealth that is indicative of an era coming to a close. The solutions adopted thus far – to pay people so little that it is cheaper to employ them than to invest in technology, or to create wasteful transactional activity that creams off wealth from truly productive work – are retrograde and self-defeating, seeking to defend a picture of human motivation that has served its time.

There is good reason for optimism. When the industrial revolution gave birth to the technology of mass production it also created the conditions for the co-operative movement, mutual and benevolent societies, universal education and the National Health Service, and the spirit that drove these social innovations still burns deep in the British psyche. All mainstream political parties speak for the values of freedom, equality of opportunity, self-determination, mutuality and the tolerance of difference. Such fine words, however, without action are bereft of meaning, and our political institutions remain committed to an economic system which, in requiring that people compete to outdo one another, must, ultimately, collapse through reciprocal destruction. Only a system that acknowledges and builds upon the innate human capacity for collaboration places no limit on the flourishing of life on earth.

INDEX